Quick and Easy Meals in Minutes

By

Carolyn Humphries

foulsham
LONDON . NEW YORK . TORONTO . SYDNEY

foulsham

The Publishing House, Bennetts Close,
Cippenham, Berks SL1 5AP, England

ISBN 0-572-02183-6

Copyright © 1995 W. Foulsham & Co. Ltd.

All rights reserved

The Copyright Act prohibits (subject to
certain very limited exceptions) the making of
copies of any copyright work or of a substantial
part of such a work, including the making of
copies by photocopying or similar process.
Written permission to make a copy or copies
must therefore normally be obtained from the
publisher in advance. It is advisable also to consult
the publisher if in any doubt as to the legality of any
copying which is to be undertaken.

Printed in Great Britain by
Cox & Wyman Ltd, Reading, Berksire.

Contents

INTRODUCTION	5
NOTES ON THE RECIPES	6
SOUPS	7
STARTERS	21
MAIN MEALS	51
FISH	52
BEEF	68
LAMB	80
PORK	94
POULTRY	108
MEATLESS MEALS	120
SNACKS & LIGHT MEALS	133
DESSERTS	145
QUICK BREADS, BISCUITS & CAKES	171
INDEX	187

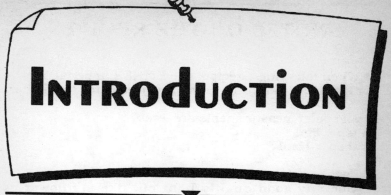

INTRODUCTION

We all seem to live life in the fast lane these days with little or no time to cook.

But for many of us, food IS important - a pleasure not just a necessity. It's no good looking at recipe books that have endless lists of unfamiliar ingredients and then, even if you scour the world for them, you discover they take an age to prepare and cook. You need a handy little tome, bursting with easy-to-prepare meals made from fresh, simple ingredients, that look and taste exquisite. And here it is!

In this book, I've created a whole range of mouth-watering starters, main courses and puds. You don't have to be a first-class chef to make them and they don't take an eternity to cook (if at all).

And if you just want a quick bite, you needn't settle for a can of beans on toast any more. There's a whole chapter on delicious snacks and one on quick bakes to set the taste buds tingling.

When you've dipped into this book a few times, I'm sure you'll agree that the most wonderful meals don't have to be difficult or time consuming to prepare. The very best are quick and easy meals in minutes!

NOTES ON THE RECIPES

* When following a recipe, use EITHER imperial, metric or American measures, never swop from one to another.

* All spoon measurements are level:
1 tsp = 5ml
1 tbsp = 15ml

* Eggs are standard (size 3) unless otherwise stated.
* Use any good quality light oil, like sunflower or groundnut (peanut) unless olive oil is specifically called for.
* All preparation and cooking times are approximate.
* Always wash and peel, if necessary, all fresh produce before use.
* Always use fresh herbs, unless dried are specifically required. You can subtitute dried herbs, but use only half the stated quantity as they are very pungent.
* Always pre-heat the oven and cook on centre shelf unless otherwise stated.

Soups

Soups are a good choice before a less substantial main course. But they also make a delicious light meal, served with crusty bread and followed by a cheese board and fresh fruit.

BORTSCH

serves 6

ingredients	Metric	Imperial	American
Sticks (ribs) celery	2	2	2
Carrots	2	2	2
Onion	1	1	1
Cooked beetroot (red beets)	350 g	12 oz	¾ lb
Beef stock	900 ml	1½ pts	3¾ cups
Wine vinegar	15 ml	1 tbsp	1 tbsp
Salt and pepper			
To garnish:			
Soured (dairy sour) cream or natural (plain) yoghurt			

method

1. Grate vegetables into a pan.
2. Add stock and vinegar, bring to the boil, reduce heat, cover and simmer for 20 minutes or until vegetables are tender.
3. Season to taste. Ladle into soup bowls and garnish each with a spoonful of soured cream or yoghurt.

note

This soup can also be served chilled.

Prep time: 10 minutes
Cook time: 20 minutes

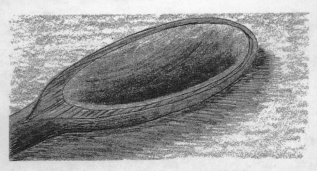

CHILLED CUCUMBER SOUP WITH DILL

serves 4

ingredients	Metric	Imperial	American
Cucumber	1	1	1
Salt			
Dried dill (dillweed)	10 ml	2 tsp	2 tsp
Cider or wine vinegar	30 ml	2 tbsp	2 tbsp
Pepper			
Natural (plain) yoghurt	300 ml	½ pt	1¼ cups
Cold milk	300 ml	½ pt	1¼ cups

method

1. Cut 4 thin slices from the cucumber and reserve for garnish. Grate remainder into a bowl.

2. Sprinkle with salt, stir and leave to stand for 10 minutes.

3. Squeeze out all the moisture and drain off.

4. Stir in dill, vinegar and a little pepper, and then add the yoghurt.

5. If time allows, chill, then stir in milk just before serving in soup bowls. Garnish with reserved slices of cucumber.

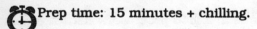Prep time: 15 minutes + chilling.

CURRIED PARSNIP SOUP

This recipe is equally good made with sweet potatoes or yams instead of parsnips.

serves 6

ingredients	Metric	Imperial	American
Parsnips, sliced	450 g	1 lb	1 lb
Onion, chopped	1	1	1
Butter or margarine	25 g	1 oz	2 tbsp
Curry powder	15 ml	1 tbsp	1 tbsp
Vegetable stock	600 ml	1 pt	2½ cups
Milk	300 ml	½ pt	1¼ cups
Salt and pepper			
Chopped parsley	15 ml	1 tbsp	1 tbsp
To serve:			
Hot Walnut Bread (P. 175)			

method

1. Put parsnips, onion and butter or margarine in a pan. Fry (sauté) gently, stirring for 3 minutes.
2. Add curry powder and fry for 1 minute.
3. Stir in stock, bring to the boil, reduce heat, cover and simmer for 15 minutes or until parsnips are really tender.
4. Blend or purée in a food processor. Return to pan.
5. Stir in milk, season to taste and add parsley. Heat through.
6. Serve ladled into soup bowls with hot walnut bread.

Prep time: 10 minutes
Cook time: 20 minutes

GOLDEN CHEDDAR SOUP

serves 4

ingredients

	Metric	Imperial	American
Large potato, diced	1	1	1
Large onion, chopped	1	1	1
Carrot, chopped	1	1	1
Celery stick (rib)	1	1	1
Vegetable or chicken stock	600 ml	1 pt	2 ¼ cups
Cheddar cheese, grated	100 g	4 oz	1 cup
Milk or single (light) cream	150 ml	¼ pt	⅔ cup
Chopped parsley	30 ml	2 tbsp	2 tbsp
Chopped (snipped) chives			

method

1. Simmer all the vegetables in the stock for 15 minutes or until soft.
2. Blend or purée in a food processor and return to pan. Stir in the cheese, milk or cream and herbs. Heat through but do not boil.
3. Serve hot.

Prep time: 10 minutes
Cook time: 15 minutes

GREEK EGG AND LEMON SOUP

serves 6

ingredients	Metric	Imperial	American
Chicken or lamb stock	900 ml	1½ pts	3¾ cups
Long-grain rice	50 g	2 oz	¼ cup
Eggs	2	2	2
Small lemon	1	1	1
Water	15 ml	1 tbsp	1 tbsp
Salt and pepper			
To garnish:			
Chopped parsley			

method

1. Put stock and rice in a pan. Bring to the boil and simmer for 10-12 minutes until rice is cooked.
2. Break eggs into a bowl. Squeeze in the juice from the lemon and add water. Whisk to blend.
3. Whisk in one ladleful of the hot stock. Then whisk in two more ladlesful.
4. Remove hot soup from heat and stir in this egg mixture. Taste and season if necessary.
5. Serve in soup bowls, garnished with chopped parsley.

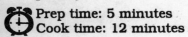
Prep time: 5 minutes
Cook time: 12 minutes

Green Velvet Soup

serves 6

ingredients	Metric	Imperial	American
Spinach	450 g	1 lb	1 lb
Butter	15 g	½ oz	1 tbsp
Onion, chopped	1	1	1
Broad (lima) beans, shelled	175 g	6 oz	1 cup
Grated nutmeg	pinch	pinch	pinch
Vegetable stock	600 ml	1 pt	2½ cups
Milk	300 ml	½ pt	1¼ cups
Salt and pepper			
To garnish:			
Croûtons			

method

1. Wash spinach well, removing any thick stalks. Tear leaves into pieces.
2. Melt butter in a pan. Add onion and fry (sauté) gently for one minute.
3. Add spinach and stir until it cooks down a little.
4. Add beans, nutmeg and stock. Bring to the boil, reduce heat, cover and simmer for 15 minutes until beans are soft.
5. Blend or purée in a food processor until smooth.
6. Return to pan and add milk. Season if necessary. Re-heat and serve in soup bowls, garnished with croûtons.

Prep time: 10 minutes
Cook time: 18 minutes

Mediterranean Summer Soup

serves 4

ingredients	Metric	Imperial	American
Slice of fresh bread	1	1	1
Oil	15 ml	1 tbsp	1 tbsp
Lemon juice	15 ml	1 tbsp	1 tbsp
Water	30 ml	2 tbsp	2 tbsp
Small onion, chopped	½	½	½
Small garlic clove	1	1	1
Red (bell) pepper, roughly diced	1	1	1
Cucumber, roughly chopped	½	½	½
Can tomatoes	400 g	14 oz	14 oz
Tomato purée (paste)	15 ml	1 tbsp	1 tbsp
Caster (superfine) sugar	5 ml	1 tsp	1 tsp
Salt and pepper			
Iced water	150 ml	¼ pt	⅔ cup
To garnish:			
Chopped parsley			

method:

1. Break up bread and place in a bowl with the oil, lemon juice and water. Leave to soak for 5 minutes.
2. Place in a blender or food processor with remaining ingredients except iced water. Run machine until smooth.
3. Stir in iced water and season.
4. Ladle into soup bowls and garnish with chopped parsley.

Prep time: 10 minutes

MINTED PEA SOUP

This soup is also good served chilled.

serves 6

ingredients	Metric	Imperial	American
Fresh peas (unshelled weight) OR	900 g	2 lb	2 lb
Frozen peas	450 g	1 lb	4 cups
Chicken stock	900 ml	1½ pts	3¾ cups
Caster (superfine) sugar	10 ml	2 tsp	2 tsp
Large sprig of mint	1	1	1
Salt and pepper			
Egg yolk	1	1	1
Single (light) cream	30 ml	2 tbsp	2 tbsp
To garnish:			
A little extra single (light) cream			

method

1. Shell peas, if using fresh. Place peas in a pan with the stock, sugar, mint and a little salt and pepper.
2. Bring to the boil, reduce heat, cover and simmer for 15 minutes. Discard mint sprig.
3. Blend or purée in a food processor until smooth.
4. Return to the pan. Blend egg yolk and cream together and stir into soup. Re-heat, but do not boil.
5. Serve in soup bowls, garnished with a swirl of cream.

Prep time: 5 minutes (15 if shelling peas)
Cook time: 15 minutes

Mushroom and Corn Chowder

serves 4

ingredients

	Metric	Imperial	American
Button mushrooms, chopped	225 g	8 oz	4 cups
Onion, chopped	1	1	1
Butter or margarine	40 g	1½ oz	3 tbsp
Plain (all-purpose) flour	25 g	1 oz	¼ cup
Chicken stock	300 ml	½ pt	1¼ cups
Milk	300 ml	½ pt	1¼ cups
Can sweetcorn (corn)	320 g	12 oz	12 oz
Single (light) cream	30 ml	2 tbsp	2 tbsp
To garnish:			
Chopped (snipped) chives			

method

1. Fry (sauté) mushrooms and onion gently in a pan with the butter or margarine for 3 minutes, stirring continually.
2. Add flour and cook stirring for a further minute.
3. Remove from heat, blend in the stock, milk and corn.
4. Return to heat, bring to the boil, stirring. Reduce heat and simmer gently for 10 minutes. Remove from heat.
5. Season to taste and stir in cream. Serve in soup bowls, garnished with chives.

Prep time: 5 minutes
Cook time: 14 minutes

PEANUT SOUP

serves 6

ingredients

	Metric	Imperial	American
Small onion chopped	1	1	1
Celery stick (rib), chopped	1	1	1
Butter	25 g	1 oz	2 tbsp
Plain (all-purpose) flour	20 g	¾ oz	1½ tbsp
Chicken stock	1 litre	1¾ pts	4¼ cups
Smooth peanut butter	225 g	8 oz	1 cup
Single (light) cream	200 ml	7 fl oz	scant 1 cup

To garnish:
Chopped peanuts
Chopped parsley

method

1. Fry (sauté) onion and celery in the butter in a pan until soft, but not brown.
2. Sprinkle in the flour and cook, stirring for 1 minute.
3. Gradually blend in the stock, bring to the boil and simmer for 5 minutes.
4. Blend or purée in a food processor.
5. Return to pan and blend in peanut butter and cream. Re-heat, but do not boil.
6. Serve in soup bowls garnished with chopped peanuts and parsley.

Prep time: 5 minutes
Cook time: 8-10 minutes

QUICK MINESTRONE

If you have a food processor, use it to grate the vegetables.

serves 6

ingredients	Metric	Imperial	American
Small onion, grated	1	1	1
Oil	15 ml	1 tbsp	1 tbsp
Carrot, grated	1	1	1
Small parsnip or turnip, grated	1	1	1
Small cabbage, shredded	¼	¼	¼
Frozen peas	50 g	2 oz	½ cup
Quick cook macaroni	25 g	1 oz	¼ cup
Can chopped tomatoes	400 g	14 oz	14 oz
Vegetable stock cube	1	1	1
Dried oregano	2.5 ml	½ tsp	½ tsp
Salt and pepper			
To serve:			
Grated Parmesan cheese			

method

1. Fry (sauté) onion in the oil in a large pan for 1 minute, stirring.
2. Add remaining ingredients. Fill tomato can with cold water and add to pan. Add a further can-full of water.
3. Bring to the boil, reduce heat and simmer for 10 minutes, or until vegetables and pasta are soft.
4. Taste and re-season if necessary.
5. Serve in soup bowls with Parmesan cheese to sprinkle over.

Prep time: 10 minutes
Cook time: 12 minutes

Watercress Soup

serves 6

ingredients

	Metric	Imperial	American
Watercress bunches	2	2	2
Onion, sliced	1	1	1
Large potato, diced	1	1	1
Butter or margarine	25 g	1 oz	2 tbsp
Chicken stock	600 ml	1 pt	2½ cups
Salt and pepper			
Milk	300 ml	½ pt	1¼ cups
To garnish:			
Soured (dairy sour) cream or natural (plain) yoghurt			

method

1. Wash watercress, cut off and discard feathery stalks and chop leaves.
2. Place in a pan with the onion, potato and butter or margarine.
3. Cook, stirring for 3 minutes.
4. Add stock, bring to the boil, reduce heat, cover and simmer gently for 15 - 20 minutes, until vegetables are soft.
5. Blend or purée in a food processor.
6. Stir in milk and season to taste.
7. Either re-heat, but do not boil, or chill. Serve in soup bowls, garnished with a spoonful of soured cream or yoghurt on each.

Prep time: 10 minutes
Cook time: 18-23 minutes

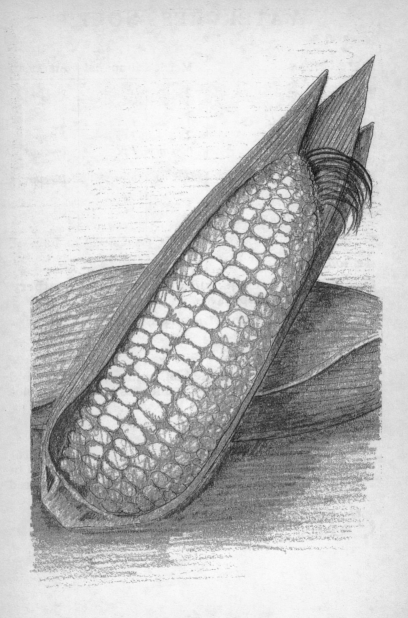

STARTERS

A sumptuous starter will set the scene for a truly memorable meal. It should be filling enough to stave off the first hunger pangs, but not so substantial as to dull the appetite for the main course. Remember to keep portions small and beautifully presented.

ASIAN PEARS WITH BLUE CHEESE MAYONNAISE

If not serving immediately, toss fruit slices in lemon juice to prevent browning. If you can't buy Asian pears, ripe dessert pears are equally delicious.

serves 6

ingredients	Metric	Imperial	American
Danish Blue cheese	100 g	4 oz	1 cup
Mayonnaise	60 ml	4 tbsp	4 tbsp
Double (heavy) cream	45 ml	3 tbsp	3 tbsp
Lemon juice	5 ml	1 tsp	1 tsp
Black pepper			
Asian pears	4 - 6	4 - 6	4 - 6
To garnish:			
Paprika and sprigs of parsley			

method

1. Crumble cheese into a bowl and mash well with 15 ml/1 tbsp of the mayonnaise.
2. When fairly smooth, beat in the remaining mayonnaise, cream and lemon juice. Add a good grinding of pepper.
3. Quarter, core and slice Asian pears, but do not peel.
4. Arrange the pear slices attractively on individual serving plates and spoon the mayonnaise to one side of the slices. Dust mayonnaise with paprika and garnish each plate with a sprig of parsley.

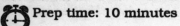 Prep time: 10 minutes

ASPARAGUS WITH FRESH HERB HOLLANDAISE

serves 4

ingredients

	Metric	Imperial	American
Asparagus	750 g	1½ lbs	1½ lbs
Sauce:			
Watercress bunch	1	1	1
Parsley sprigs	4	4	4
Marjoram leaves	8	8	8
Eggs	2	2	2
Lemon juice	30 ml	2 tbsp	2 tbsp
Butter, melted	100 g	4 oz	½ cup

method

1. Wash asparagus. Trim off about 5 cm/2 in from base of stems. Tie spears in a bundle.

2. Stand bundle in a pan of lightly salted water. Cover with a lid (or foil if pan is not deep enough).

3. Bring to the boil, reduce heat and cook over a moderate heat for 10 minutes. Turn off heat and leave for 5 minutes. Drain.

4. Meanwhile make sauce. Cut off watercress stalks. Wash leaves and chop finely with the parsley and marjoram.

5. Whisk eggs in a pan with the lemon juice. Gradually whisk in melted butter. Cook over a gentle heat, whisking all the time until thickened. DO NOT BOIL. Stir in herbs.

6. Lay asparagus on warm plates, spoon a little sauce in a line over stalks just below the heads. Serve straight away.

Prep time: 15 minutes
Cook time: 10 minutes

Aubergine Dip

serves 6

ingredients

	Metric	Imperial	American
Large aubergine (eggplant)	1	1	1
Lemon juice	5 ml	1 tsp	1 tsp
Natural (plain) yoghurt	30 ml	2 tbsp	2 tbsp
Small onion, finely chopped	1	1	1
Low fat soft cheese	175 g	6 oz	¾ cup
Chopped (snipped) chives	5 ml	1 tsp	1 tsp
Salt and pepper			
To serve:			
French bread			

method

1. Cut stalk off aubergine and discard. Boil in water for 10 minutes until tender.

2. Drain. Peel off purple skin and sieve or blend flesh with the lemon juice and yoghurt.

3. Beat in the onion, cheese and chives and season to taste.

4. Chill, if time, then serve with French bread.

Prep time: 10 minutes + chill time if possible
Cook time: 10 minutes

AVOCADO SOUTH AMERICAN-STYLE

serves 4

ingredients	Metric	Imperial	American
Ripe avocados	2	2	2
Lemon juice	30 ml	2 tbsp	2 tbsp
Worcestershire sauce	30 ml	2 tbsp	2 tbsp
Small garlic clove, crushed	1	1	1
Chilli (chili) powder	1.5 ml	¼ tsp	¼ tsp
Olive oil	60 ml	4 tbsp	4 tbsp
Salt and pepper			
Cucumber piece	5 cm	2 in	2 in
Tomatoes, chopped	2	2	2
To serve:			
Hot toast or tortilla chips			

method

1. Halve avocados, remove stones (pits) and scoop flesh into a bowl.

2. Mash well with lemon juice then work in Worcestershire sauce, garlic and chilli powder.

3. Add the oil, a little at a time, beating well after each addition.

4. Season to taste and stir in the cucumber and tomato.

5. Pile onto plates or into ramekins (custard pots) and serve with hot toast or tortilla chips.

Prep time: 10 minutes

BRITTANY ARTICHOKES

serves 4

ingredients	Metric	Imperial	American
Globe artichokes	4	4	4
Lemon juice	2	2	2
Dipping sauce:			
Butter	50 g	2 oz	¼ cup
Soft garlic and herb cheese	100 g	4 oz	½ cup
Milk	60 ml	4 tbsp	4 tbsp

method

1. Twist off the artichoke stalks and trim bases level so they will stand up. Trim off points of outer leaves, if preferred, with scissors (this is not strictly necessary).

2. Cook in boiling water to which the lemon juice has been added for about 20 minutes or until a leaf pulls away easily. Drain and turn upside down on kitchen paper for a few minutes. Transfer to serving plates.

3. Meanwhile make dipping sauce: melt butter and cheese in a pan, stirring over a moderate heat. Gradually blend in the milk and heat through, stirring until smooth. Pour into 4 little individual dishes and serve with artichokes.

to eat:

Pull off each leaf in turn, dip the base in the sauce and draw through the teeth to remove the fleshy part. When the hairy choke is revealed, cut or pull it off and eat the heart with a knife and fork and any remaining sauce.

Prep time: 10 minutes
Cook time: 20 minutes

CALAMARES A LA PLANCHA

Contrary to popular belief, small squid, or calamares, are not chewy, but tender and full of flavour when cooked in this way.

serves 4

ingredients	Metric	Imperial	American
Onion, chopped	1	1	1
Garlic clove, finely chopped	2	2	2
Olive oil	60 ml	4 tbsp	4 tbsp
Small squid, cleaned and sliced into rings	450 g	1 lb	1 lb
Salt and pepper			
Chopped parsley	30 ml	2 tbsp	2 tbsp
To serve:			
Lemon wedges and crusty bread			

method

1. Gently fry (sauté) onion and garlic in the oil for 2 minutes until soft but not brown.

2. Add squid (including tentacles) and toss gently until rings turn pinky-white.

3. Season with salt and pepper, cover pan with a lid and cook over a very gentle heat for 5-10 minutes. The squid will now be bathed in lots of delicious juice.

4. Sprinkle with chopped parsley, then spoon into warm shallow dishes and serve with lots of lemon wedges and crusty bread to mop up the juices.

Prep time: 5 - 10 minutes plus cleaning squid, if necessary
Cook time: 10 - 15 minutes

CHINESE-STYLE SALAD

This also makes a delicious summer lunch dish. Try it with canned tuna for a change.

serves 4 - 6

ingredients	Metric	Imperial	American
Beansprouts	175 g	6 oz	3 cups
Red (bell) pepper, chopped	½	½	½
Peeled prawns (shrimp)	100 g	4 oz	⅔ cup
Dressing:			
Soy sauce	10 ml	2 tsp	2 tsp
White vinegar	10 ml	2 tsp	2 tsp
Caster (superfine) sugar	5 ml	1 tsp	1 tsp
Olive or sesame oil	30 ml	2 tbsp	2 tbsp
Salt and pepper			
To garnish:			
Lettuce leaves chopped and spring onion (scallion)			

method

1. Wash beansprouts and put in a bowl with the chopped pepper and prawns.
2. Blend dressing ingredients together and pour over the beansprouts. Toss well.
3. Pile onto lettuce leaves and garnish with a little chopped spring onion.

 Prep time: 5 minutes

Cottage Avocado

serves 6

ingredients	Metric	Imperial	American
Ripe avocados	3	3	3
Lemon juice			
Cottage cheese with prawns (shrimp)	225 g	8 oz	1 cup
Jar Danish lumpfish roe	50 g	2 oz	2 oz
To garnish:			
Lemon wedges			

method

1. Halve avocados, remove stones (pits) and place each half on an individual dish. Brush with lemon juice to prevent discolouration.

2. Spoon cottage cheese with prawns into the cavities and top each with a spoonful of lumpfish roe.

3. Garnish each dish with a wedge of lemon. Serve straight away.

 Prep time: 5 minutes

Creamy Cucumber with Crab

Substitute prawns (shrimp) for crab if you prefer. This recipe also makes a delicious light lunch or supper dish, served on a bed of plain boiled rice.

serves 4 - 6

ingredients	Metric	Imperial	American
Large cucumber, diced	1	1	1
Butter	50 g	2 oz	¼ cup
Button mushrooms, sliced	175 g	6 oz	3 cups
Plain (all-purpose) flour	10 ml	2 tsp	2 tsp
Chicken stock	150 ml	¼ pt	⅔ cup
Sherry	15 ml	1 tbsp	1 tbsp
Single (light) cream	90 ml	6 tbsp	6 tbsp
White crabmeat	100 g	4 oz	½ cup
Salt and pepper			
To garnish:			
Chopped parsley			
To serve:			
Hot Walnut Bread (p.175) or Savoury Wholemeal Rolls (p.179)			

method

1. Cook cucumber in boiling, lightly salted water for 3 minutes. Drain, rinse with cold water and drain again.

2. Melt butter in a pan, add mushrooms and cook, stirring for 2 minutes.

3. Add cucumber, cover with a lid and cook gently for 2 minutes.

4. Blend in the flour, then gradually stir in the stock, sherry and cream until smooth.

5. Bring to the boil, stirring. Add crab meat and heat through.

6. Spoon into scallop shells or ramekins (custard cups), garnish with chopped parsley and serve with Hot Walnut Bread or Savoury Wholemeal Rolls.

Prep time: 10 minutes
Cook time: 10 minutes

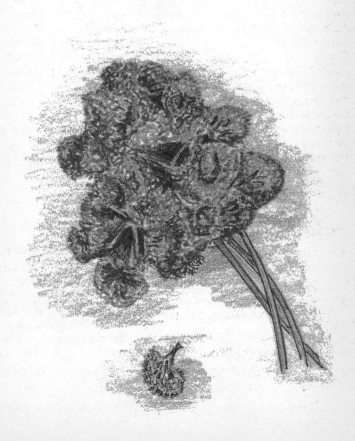

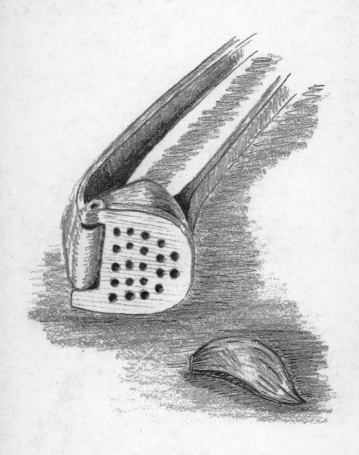

Garlicky Mushroo[ms]

serves 4

ingredients	Metric	Imperial	
Large, flat mushrooms	8	8	8
Butter	25 g	1 oz	2 tbsp
Large garlic clove, finely chopped	1	1	1
Salt and pepper			
Dry white wine	150 ml	¼ pt	⅔ cup
Single (light) cream or natural (plain) yoghurt	150 ml	¼ pt	⅔ cup
To garnish: Chopped parsley			
To serve: French bread			

method

1. Wash mushrooms, pat dry on kitchen paper. Peel if necessary.
2. Grease a large ovenproof dish with the butter.
3. Lay mushrooms in the dish, stalks up.
4. Scatter garlic over, season with a little salt and pepper, and pour over the wine and cream. Cover with foil.
5. Bake at 190°C/375°F/gas mark 5 for about 20 minutes until mushrooms are tender.
6. Transfer mushrooms to serving plates, spoon sauce over and sprinkle with chopped parsley. Serve with French bread to mop up juices.

Prep time: 5 minutes
Cook time: 20 minutes

GOLDEN CAMEMBERT WITH CRANBERRY SAUCE

This recipe is equally delicious with small portions of goat's cheese.

serves 6

ingredients	Metric	Imperial	American
Individual Camembert portions	6	6	6
Eggs, beaten	2	2	2
Fresh white breadcrumbs	50 g	2 oz	1 cup
Oil for deep-frying			
To garnish:			
Salad			
To serve:			
Cranberry sauce			

method

1. Dip cheese portions in beaten egg then breadcrumbs. Repeat to coat thoroughly.

2. Heat oil until a cube of day-old bread browns in 30 seconds. Fry cheeses for 2 minutes or until crisp and golden brown.

3. Drain on kitchen paper and transfer to serving plates. Add an attractive salad garnish and spoon a little cranberry sauce to the side of each cheese. Serve immediately.

Prep time: 10 minutes
Cook time: 2 minutes

Jellied Eggs en Cocotte

For this dish, the egg yolks should be soft cooked, but if you don't like them this way, cook them for 2 minutes more.

serves 4

ingredients	Metric	Imperial	American
Eggs	4	4	4
Streaky bacon rashers (slices)	4	4	4
Can condensed beef consommé, chilled	300 g	11 oz	11 oz
To garnish:			
Chopped parsley			
To serve:			
Hot crusty bread			

method

1. Boil eggs for 4 minutes for soft yolks and firm whites. Drain and place in cold water immediately to prevent further cooking.

2. Meanwhile grill (broil) or fry (sauté) bacon until crisp. Cut into bite-sized pieces.

3. Carefully shell eggs and place in 4 ramekins (custard cups). Add the bacon.

4. Spoon jellied consomme over each and decorate with chopped parsley. Chill if you have time before serving with hot crusty bread.

Prep time: 5 minutes, plus chilling
Cook time: 4 - 6 minutes

Moorish Mushrooms

Serves 4 - 6

ingredients	Metric	Imperial	American
Button mushrooms	450 g	1 lb	1 lb
Onion, chopped	1	1	1
Garlic clove, crushed	1	1	1
Olive oil	60 ml	4 tbsp	4 tbsp
Can chopped tomatoes	400 g	14 oz	14 oz
Caster (superfine) sugar	5 ml	1 tsp	1 tsp
Red wine	150 ml	1/4 pt	2/3 cup
To garnish: Chopped parsley **To serve:** Ciabatta or French bread			

method

1. Put mushrooms, onion, garlic and oil in a pan and cook, gently, stirring for 3 minutes.

2. Add tomatoes, sugar and wine. Bring to the boil, reduce heat and simmer for 15 minutes or until liquid is well reduced.

3. Season to taste and serve hot or chilled, sprinkled with chopped parsley, with Ciabatta or French bread.

Prep time: 5 minutes
Cook time: 18 minutes

Melon and Clementine Cocktail

serves 6

ingredients	Metric	Imperial	American
Honeydew melon	1	1	1
Clementines	3	3	3
Pieces of stem ginger in syrup, chopped	2	2	2
Sherry	45 ml	3 tbsp	3 tbsp
To serve:			
Hot Herb Loaf (p.174)			

method

1. Cut melon in half, remove seeds then scoop out flesh with a melon baller or cut into dice. Place in a bowl.
2. Peel and segment clementines, discarding any pith. Add to bowl.
3. Mix in ginger, 30 ml/2 tbsp of the ginger syrup and the sherry. Toss well. Chill, if time, before serving in individual glass dishes.

 Prep time: 10 minutes

MELON WITH WESTPHALIAN HAM

You can use any of the raw cured hams for this recipe, but Westphalian is usually a very good buy.

serves 4

ingredients	Metric	Imperial	American
Honeydew melon	1	1	1
Westphalian ham slices	4	4	4
Pickled gherkins (cornichons)	4	4	4
To serve:			
Pumpernickel			

method

1. Halve melon, scoop out seeds, cut each half into 4 wedges and peel them.
2. Cut each slice of ham in half lengthwise and wrap each round a wedge of melon.
3. Lay these on 4 individual serving plates.
4. Using a sharp knife, make four slices down each gherkin from the stalk end almost down to the base then gently ease slices apart to form a fan.
5. Lay one on each plate to garnish and serve with Pumpernickel.

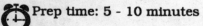Prep time: 5 - 10 minutes

Moules Marinières

serves 4 - 6

ingredients	Metric	Imperial	American
Mussels	1.75 kg	4 lb	4 lb
Butter	40 g	1½ oz	3 tbsp
Large onion, chopped	1	1	1
Wineglass dry white wine or vermouth	2	2	2
Wineglass water	1	1	1
Black pepper			
Chopped parsley	30 ml	2 tbsp	2 tbsp
To serve:			
French bread			

method

1. Scrub mussels and scrape off beards and barnacles. Discard any that are damaged or do not close immediately when tapped. Rinse well in cold running water.

2. Heat butter in a large pan. Fry (sauté) onion gently for one minute without browning.

3. Add mussels, wine and water and a grinding of pepper. Bring to the boil, cover pan and shake over a moderate heat for 5 minutes.

4. Discard any mussels that have not opened. Ladle into soup bowls with the liquor and sprinkle liberally with chopped parsley.

5. Serve with lots of crusty bread to mop up the juices.

Prep time: 10-15 minutes
Cook time: 6 minutes

MOZZARELLA AND TOMATOES WITH BASIL

Do not attempt to use dried basil for this dish - it just will not taste the same.

serves 4

ingredients	Metric	Imperial	American
Beefsteak tomatoes, sliced	4	4	4
Mozzarella cheese, sliced	225 g	8 oz	2 cups
Basil leaves	16	16	16
Olive oil	60 ml	4 tbsp	4 tbsp
Black pepper			
To serve:			
Ciabatta or French bread			

method

1. Arrange tomato and mozzarella slices attractively on 4 serving plates.
2. Tear up basil leaves and sprinkle over.
3. Drizzle with oil and give a good grinding of black pepper.
4. Serve with Ciabatta or French bread.

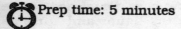 Prep time: 5 minutes

Mushroom Pâté

serves 4

ingredients

	Metric	Imperial	American
Butter or margarine	25 g	1 oz	2 tbsp
Small onion, finely chopped	1	1	1
Mushrooms, finely chopped	350 g	12 oz	6 cups
Lemon juice	15 ml	1 tbsp	1 tbsp
Low fat soft cheese	225 g	8 oz	1 cup
Chopped parsley	30 ml	2 tbsp	2 tbsp
To serve:			
Hot buttered toast			

method

1. Melt butter in a pan. Fry (sauté) onion until pale golden.

2. Add mushrooms, fry until no liquid remains, stirring all the time.

3. Add lemon juice, turn into a bowl and allow to cool.

4. Beat in the cheese and parsley. Chill, if time, before serving with hot buttered toast.

Prep time: 10 minutes, plus chilling if possible
Cook time: about 8 minutes

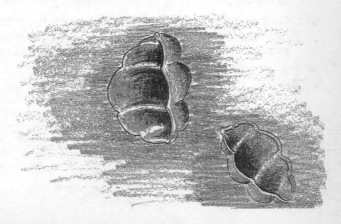

PÂTÉ-STUFFED PEPPERS

Choose (bell) peppers of even size and shape for this recipe.

serves 6

ingredients	Metric	Imperial	American
Green (bell) pepper	1	1	1
Red or yellow (bell) pepper	1	1	1
Smooth liver pâté	225 g	8 oz	1 cup
Soft white breadcrumbs	25 g	1 oz	½ cup
Butter, melted	50 g	2 oz	¼ cup
Chopped (snipped) chives	15 ml	1 tbsp	1 tbsp
Black pepper			
To garnish:			
Salad			

method

1. Cut stalk ends off peppers and remove seeds.

2. Blend pâté with the breadcrumbs, melted butter, herbs and a little black pepper until smooth.

3. Pack into peppers, wrap in cling film (plastic wrap) and chill for at least 30 minutes until filling has firmed up.

4. Cut each pepper into 6 slices, carefully transfer one of each colour to individual serving plates and garnish with a little salad before serving.

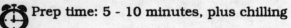
Prep time: 5 - 10 minutes, plus chilling

PEARS WITH CREAMY TARRAGON DRESSING

serves 6

ingredients

	Metric	Imperial	American
Ripe pears	6	6	6
Lettuce leaves			
Dressing:			
Crème fraîche	150 ml	¼ pt	⅔ cup
Sunflower oil	30 ml	2 tbsp	2 tbsp
Lemon juice	10 ml	2 tsp	2 tsp
Chopped tarragon	30 ml	2 tbsp	2 tbsp
Caster (superfine) sugar	5 ml	1 tsp	1 tsp
Salt and pepper			
To garnish:			
Small tarragon sprigs			

method

1. Peel, halve and core pears. Place cut-side down on a bed of lettuce on individual serving plates.
2. Beat dressing ingredients together and spoon over pears. Chill, if time, before serving garnished with small sprigs of tarragon.

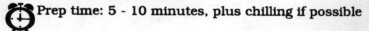 Prep time: 5 - 10 minutes, plus chilling if possible

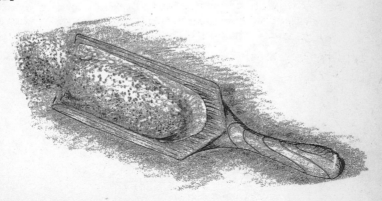

PINEAPPLE BOATS

serves 4

ingredients	Metric	Imperial	American
Small fresh pineapple	1	1	1
Cottage cheese	225 g	8 oz	1 cup
Walnuts, chopped	50 g	2 oz	½ cup
Salt and pepper			

method

1. Cut pineapple in quarters, lengthwise, leaving green leaves on.
2. Cut most of the flesh off skin leaving a thin border of fruit.
3. Roughly chop, discarding any hard core.
4. Mix chopped fruit with the cottage cheese and walnuts. Season to taste and spoon back into skins.
5. Chill, if time, before serving.

Prep time: 5 - 10 minutes, plus chilling if possible

Rosy Eggs

serves 4

ingredients

ingredients	Metric	Imperial	American
Eggs, hard boiled (hard-cooked)	4	4	4
Mayonnaise	15 ml	1 tbsp	1 tbsp
Tomato purée (paste)	10 ml	2 tsp	2 tsp
Salt and pepper			
To garnish:			
Anchovies			
Stuffed olives, sliced			
To serve:			
Lettuce			
Garlic Bread (p.173)			

method

1. Shell eggs, cut into halves, scoop out yolks and place in a bowl.
2. Mash yolks, then beat in mayonnaise, tomato purée and salt and pepper to taste.
3. Pile back into egg whites. Garnish each with a rolled anchovy fillet and a slice of stuffed olive.
4. Serve on a bed of lettuce with Garlic Bread.

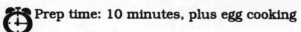 Prep time: 10 minutes, plus egg cooking

ROYAL GRAPEFRUIT

serves 6

ingredients

	Metric	Imperial	American
Grapefruit	3	3	3
Caster (superfine) sugar	30 ml	2 tbsp	2 tbsp
Port or sweet sherry	30 ml	2 tbsp	2 tbsp
Stilton cheese	75 g	3 oz	¾ cup

method

1. Cut grapefruits into halves. Loosen segments with a knife, removing any pips. Place in 6 flameproof dishes.
2. Sprinkle with sugar then port or sherry.
3. Crumble cheese and scatter over each half.
4. Place under a hot grill (broiler) for about 4 minutes until cheese has melted and is turning golden.

Prep time: 8 - 10 minutes
Cook time: 4 minutes

Smoked Mackerel with Horseradish Mayonnaise

serves 4

ingredients

	Metric	Imperial	American
Mayonnaise	60 ml	4 tbsp	4 tbsp
Olive oil	15 ml	1 tbsp	1 tbsp
Creamed horseradish	15 ml	1 tbsp	1 tbsp
Smoked mackerel fillets	4	4	4
To garnish:			
Lemon wedges			
Parsley sprigs			
To serve:			
Brown bread and butter			

method

1. Beat mayonnaise with the olive oil and horseradish to taste.
2. Lay mackerel fillets on 4 individual serving plates.
3. Spoon mayonnaise in a band across each fillet and garnish with a lemon wedge and sprig of parsley. Serve with brown bread and butter.

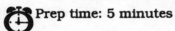

Prep time: 5 minutes

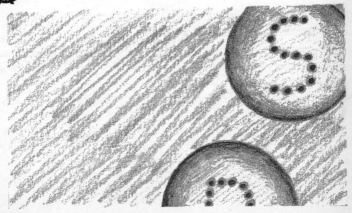

SMOKED SALMON PÂTÉ

Ask for smoked salmon pieces at your local delicatessen. They're much cheaper than slices.

serves 6

ingredients	Metric	Imperial	American
Smoked salmon pieces	225 g	8 oz	1/2 lb
Double (heavy) cream	150 ml	1/4 pt	2/3 cup
Butter, softened	50 g	2 oz	1/4 cup
Lemon juice	30 ml	2 tbsp	2 tbsp
Cayenne	pinch	pinch	pinch
To garnish:			
Lemon wedges			
Parsley sprigs			
To serve:			
Hot toast			

method

1. Discard any skin and bones from salmon.
2. Turn on blender or food processor and drop in salmon pieces, a few at a time, with the cream.
3. Add butter, a knob at a time and blend until smooth.
4. Add lemon juice and cayenne and run machine briefly again. Chill if time.
5. Spoon on to individual serving plates, garnish each with a wedge of lemon and a sprig of parsley and serve with hot toast.

Prep time: 5 - 10 minutes, plus chilling if possible

SWEET 'N SOUR RUNNER BEANS

Substitute half the quantity of whole French beans if runner beans are not available.

serves 6

ingredients	Metric	Imperial	American
Runner beans	900 g	2 lb	2 lb
Streaky bacon rashers (slices), diced	6	6	6
Button mushrooms, sliced	100 g	4 oz	2 cups
Olive oil	30 ml	2 tbsp	2 tbsp
Worcestershire sauce	30 ml	2 tbsp	2 tbsp
Soy sauce	15 ml	1 tbsp	1 tbsp
Soft light brown sugar	30 ml	2 tbsp	2 tbsp
Wine vinegar	30 ml	2 tbsp	2 tbsp

method

1. String and slice beans and cook in boiling salted water for about 5 minutes until just tender. Drain.
2. In a large pan quickly fry (sauté) bacon and mushrooms in the oil until golden. Remove from pan with a draining spoon.
3. Add remaining ingredients to juices in pan. Stir until sugar dissolves, then bring to the boil.
4. Add bacon, mushrooms and beans. Toss over a gently heat until heated through.
5. Serve straight away.

Prep time: 15 minutes
Cook time: 8 - 10 minutes

TANGY WHITING GOUJONS

serves 6

ingredients	Metric	Imperial	American
Whiting fillets, skinned	750 g	1½ lb	1½ lb
Plain (all-purpose) flour	25 g	1 oz	¼ cup
Salt and pepper			
Eggs, beaten	2	2	2
Fresh breadcrumbs	175 g	6 oz	3 cups
Mayonnaise	150 ml	¼ pt	⅔ cup
Lime, grated rind and juice	1	1	1
Oil for frying			
To garnish:			
Lime wedges			

method

1. Cut fish into strips, discarding any bones. Toss in flour seasoned with salt and pepper.

2. Coat in beaten egg, then breadcrumbs.

3. Reserve a pinch of lime rind for garnish then blend mayonnaise with rest of the lime rind and juice. Spoon into a small pot, sprinkle with reserved lime rind.

4. Heat oil until a cube of day-old bread browns in 30 seconds and deep-fry fish for 4 minutes until golden.

5. Drain on kitchen paper, arrange on a dish around pot of mayonnaise and garnish with wedges of lime.

Prep time: 15 minutes
Cook time: 4 minutes

Main Meals

This section has been divided into recipes for the different meats, poultry, fish and vegetarian options. They're all simple enough to serve any day of the week. The more elegant ones are also ideal for entertaining. But the most inportant thing they all have in common is that they are incredibly quick to make.

Fish

Fish is by nature, comparatively quick to cook which makes it ideal for inclusion in this book.

Many of the recipes in this section would also make good starters, served in smaller portions.

BAKED STUFFED PLAICE

Use a food processor, if liked, to make the stuffing by just adding the ingredients one by one to the bowl while running the machine.

serves 4

ingredients	Metric	Imperial	American
Stuffing:			
Button mushrooms, finely chopped	100 g	4 oz	2 cups
Butter	25 g	1 oz	2 tbsp
Fresh breadcrumbs	50 g	2 oz	1 cup
Chopped parsley	15 ml	1 tbsp	1 tbsp
Salt and pepper			
Plaice fillets	4	4	4
Single (light) cream	150 ml	¼ pt	⅔ cup
To garnish:			
Parsley			
To serve:			
Sautéed potatoes, broccoli			

method

1. Fry (sauté) mushrooms in the butter for 2 minutes, stirring. Add breadcrumbs, parsley and a little salt and pepper.

2. Remove dark skin from plaice fillets (do not worry about white skinned ones). Cut fillets in half lengthwise.

3. Divide stuffing among fillets. Fold over into three to encase filling.

4. Transfer to 4 individual ovenproof dishes. Spoon cream over. Cover with foil.

5. Bake in a moderate oven, 180°C/350°F/gas mark 4 for 20 minutes until cooked through. Garnish with parsley, broccoli. Serve with sautéed potatoes.

Prep time: 10 minutes
Cook time: 20 minutes

BUTTERY MACKEREL

serves 4

ingredients	Metric	Imperial	American
Whole mackerel, cleaned	4	4	4
Salt and pepper			
Butter	65 g	2½ oz	5 tbsp
Oil	15 ml	1 tbsp	1 tbsp
English mustard, made	10 ml	2 tsp	2 tsp
Caster (superfine) sugar	2.5 ml	½ tsp	½ tsp
Lemon juice	5 ml	1 tsp	1 tsp
To garnish:			
Parsley sprigs			
To serve:			
New potatoes			
Broad (lima) beans			

method

1. Cut heads off mackerel if you prefer, wipe inside and out with kitchen paper. Slash fish in several places along each side with a sharp knife and season with salt and pepper.

2. Heat 15 g/½ oz/1 tbsp butter with the oil in a large frying pan (skillet).

3. Add fish and fry (sauté) for about 5 minutes on each side until browned and cooked through.

4. Meanwhile beat remaining butter with the mustard, sugar, a little salt and pepper and the lemon juice. Shape into 4 neat pieces.

5. Remove fish from pan, drain on kitchen paper and transfer to warm serving plates.

6. Top each fish with a piece of the mustard butter and garnish with parsley. Serve with new potatoes and broad beans.

Prep time: 10 minutes
Cook time: 10 minutes

Cod Provençale

serves 4

ingredients	Metric	Imperial	American
Olive oil	15 ml	1 tbsp	1 tbsp
Onion, chopped	1	1	1
Garlic clove, crushed	1 - 2	1 - 2	1 - 2
Red (bell) pepper, sliced	1	1	1
Can chopped tomatoes	400 g	14 oz	14 oz
Tomato purée (paste)	15 ml	1 tbsp	1 tbsp
Cod fillet, skinned and cubed	450 g	1 lb	good 3 cups
Salt and pepper			
To garnish:			
Chopped parsley			
Black olives			
To serve:			
Plain boiled rice			
Mixed salad			

method

1. Put oil in a pan with onion and garlic and cook, stirring for 2 minutes until softened but not browned.
2. Add pepper and fry (sauté) for one minute.
3. Stir in tomatoes and purée, bring to the boil and boil rapidly for 5 minutes, stirring occasionally.
4. Add cod and cook gently for 3 - 5 minutes until fish is cooked but not breaking up.
5. Season to taste and serve on a bed of boiled rice, garnished with chopped parsley and black olives, with a mixed salad to follow.

Prep time: 10 minutes
Cook time: 10-15 minutes

Fish Creole

serves 4

ingredients	Metric	Imperial	American
Small white fish fillets, skinned	4	4	4
Plain (all-purpose) flour	30ml	2 tbsp	2 tbsp
Salt and pepper			
Chilli (chili) powder	2.5 ml	½ tsp	½ tsp
Butter	25 g	1 oz	2 tbsp
Oil	30 ml	2 tbsp	2 tbsp
Bananas	2	2	2
To garnish:			
Lime or lemon wedges			
To serve:			
Wild rice			
Green salad			

method

1. Dust fish with flour mixed with a little salt and pepper and the chilli powder.

2. Melt half the butter and oil in a frying pan (skillet) and fry (sauté) fish for 3 minutes on each side until lightly golden and cooked through.

3. Transfer to a warm serving dish and keep warm.

4. Fry halved bananas in remaining butter and oil until softening (about 2 minutes). Transfer to the serving dish. Garnish with lime or lemon wedges and serve hot with wild rice and green salad.

Prep time: 5 minutes
Cook time: 8 minutes

FISH AND POTATO FRY

serves 4

ingredients

	Metric	Imperial	American
Butter or margarine	15 g	½ oz	1 tbsp
Oil	15 ml	1 tbsp	1 tbsp
White fish fillet, skinned and cubed	450 g	1 lb	good 3 cups
Potatoes, grated	450 g	1 lb	4 cups
Salt and pepper			
Can tomatoes	400 g	14 oz	14 oz
Tomato purée (paste)	15 ml	1 tbsp	1 tbsp
Granulated sugar	5 ml	1 tsp	1 tsp
To serve:			
Peas			

method

1. Melt butter and oil in a medium-sized frying pan (skillet).
2. Add half the potatoes and press down well. Season.
3. Add fish in a layer, then top with remaining potatoes, press down and season.
4. Cover with a lid or foil and cook gently for 30 minutes until cooked through.
5. Meanwhile sieve or blend tomatoes until smooth. Heat in a pan with tomato purée, sugar and a little pepper.
6. Turn fish and potato fry out onto warmed serving plate. Serve cut into wedges with the tomato sauce and peas.

Prep time: 10 minutes
Cook time: 30 minutes

HEARTY FISH STEW

serves 4

ingredients	Metric	Imperial	American
Onion, thinly sliced	1	1	1
Carrots, thinly sliced	1	1	1
Large potatoes, diced	2	2	2
Large parsnip, diced	1	1	1
Small cabbage, shredded	¼	¼	¼
Butter or margarine	25 g	1 oz	2 tbsp
Can chopped tomatoes	400 g	14 oz	14 oz
Water	300 ml	½ pt	1¼ cups
Anchovy essence (extract)	5 ml	1 tsp	1 tsp
White fish, skinned and cubed	350 g	12 oz	scant 2½ cups
To garnish: Chopped parsley **To serve:** Crusty bread			

method

1. Place prepared vegetables in a large pan with butter or margarine. Fry (sauté) over a gentle heat, stirring occasionally, for 5 minutes.

2. Add tomatoes, water and anchovy essence. Bring to the boil, reduce heat, cover and simmer for 15 minutes.

3. Add fish and simmer for a further 5 minutes or until cooked.

4. Season to taste then spoon into warm bowls, sprinkle with chopped parsley and serve with crusty bread.

Prep time: 10 - 15 minutes
Cook time: 25 minutes

Quick Kedgeree

serves 4

ingredients	Metric	Imperial	American
Long-grain rice	225 g	8 oz	1 cup
Turmeric	5 ml	1 tsp	1 tsp
Smoked fish fillet (haddock, cod etc)	225 g	8 oz	½ lb
Hard boiled (hard cooked) eggs, roughly cut up	3	3	3
Single (light) cream or evaporated milk	45 ml	3 tbsp	3 tbsp
Salt and pepper			
Grated nutmeg			
To garnish:			
Chopped parsley			
To serve:			
Tomato salad			

method

1. Cook rice in boiling, lightly salted water to which the turmeric has been added, for 10 minutes or until just cooked. Drain and return to the saucepan.

2. Meanwhile skin fish and poach in water until it flakes easily with a fork (5 - 10 minutes). Drain.

3. Break up fish, discarding any bones. Add to the rice with the eggs, parsley and seasonings.

4. Stir in cream or evaporated milk and heat through.

5. Garnish with chopped parsley. Serve with tomato salad.

Prep time: 10 minutes
Cook time: 12 minutes

SALMON PARCELS

serves 4

ingredients	Metric	Imperial	American
Small salmon steaks	4	4	4
Filo pastry sheets	4	4	4
Melted butter	15 g	½ oz	1 tbsp
Tomatoes, skinned	2	2	2
Mushrooms, chopped	2	2	2
Mixed dried herbs	1.5ml	¼ tsp	¼ tsp
Quick Hollandaise sauce:			
Eggs	2	2	2
Lemon juice	30 ml	2 tbsp	2 tbsp
Cayenne	pinch	pinch	pinch
Melted butter	100 g	4 oz	½ cup
To garnish:			
Parsley sprigs			
To serve:			
New potatoes			
Mangetout (snow peas)			

method

1. Remove any skin and bones from fish.
2. Brush pastry sheets with a very little melted butter, fold in half and brush again.
3. Put a salmon steak in centre of each piece of pastry. Mix tomato and mushrooms with herbs and spoon on top.
4. Draw pastry up over filling and squeeze together to form a pouch.
5. Transfer to a lightly buttered baking sheet and brush with remaining butter. Bake in a hot oven, 200°C/400°F/gas mark 6 for about 10 - 15 minutes until golden.
6. Meanwhile make sauce: whisk eggs in a small pan with lemon juice and cayenne. Gradually whisk in butter then cook over a gentle heat, whisking all

the time until mixture thickens. DO NOT BOIL. Taste and season if necessary.

7. Transfer salmon parcels to warm serving plates, spoon a little sauce to one side, garnish with parsley and serve with new potatoes and mangetout.

Prep time: 15 - 20 minutes
Cook time 10 - 15 minutes

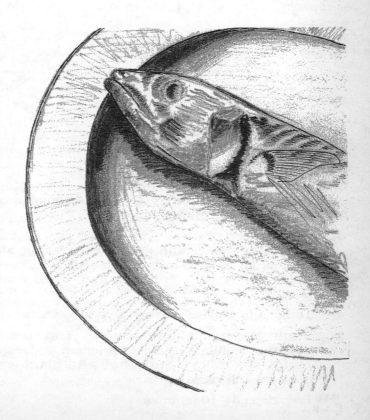

Saucy Smoked Mackerel

serves 4

ingredients	Metric	Imperial	American
Sauce:			
Butter or margarine	40 g	1½ oz	3 tbsp
Plain (all-purpose) flour	20 g	¾ oz	2½ tbsp
Milk	300 ml	½ pt	1¼ cups
Lemon, grated rind and juice	½	½	½
Horseradish relish	15 ml	1 tbsp	1 tbsp
Salt and pepper			
Smoked mackerel fillets	4	4	4
To garnish:			
Lemon wedges			
Parsley sprigs			
To serve:			
Plain boiled potatoes			
Green beans			

method

1. To make the sauce: put half the butter or margarine in a saucepan with flour and milk. Bring to the boil, whisking all the time until smooth.

2. Stir in lemon rind, horseradish and seasoning to taste. Cover with a circle of wet greaseproof (waxed) paper to prevent skin forming.

3. Put mackerel fillets on grill (broiler) pan. Dot with remaining butter and drizzle with lemon juice. Grill (broil) for 3 - 5 minutes on each side, basting occasionally with juices in pan, until cooked through.

4. Transfer to warmed serving dish, keep warm.

5. Strain juices and add to sauce. Heat through. Spoon over fish, garnish with lemon wedges and sprigs of parsley. Serve hot with plain boiled potatoes and green beans.

Prep time: 5 - 10 minutes
Cook time: 10 - 15 minutes

SWORDFISH OR TUNA STEAKS PAYSANNE

serves 4

ingredients	Metric	Imperial	American
Swordfish or tuna steaks, skinned	4	4	4
Olive oil	15 ml	1 tbsp	1 tbsp
Butter	15 g	½ oz	1 tbsp
Garlic clove, chopped	1	1	1
Chopped parsley	15 ml	1 tbsp	1 tbsp
Salt and pepper			
To garnish:			
Lemon wedges			
To serve:			
Sautéed potatoes			
French beans			

method

1. Fry (sauté) fish in the oil and butter for 5 minutes on one side until golden.

2. Turn over. Sprinkle with garlic and parsley, a good grinding of pepper and a little salt. Cover with foil or a lid and continue cooking for 5 minutes or until cooked through.

3. Garnish with lemon wedges. Serve with sautéed potatoes and French beans.

Prep time: 5 minutes
Cook time: 10 minutes (approx)

Tandoori Fish

This also makes a delicious starter for 8 people.

serves 4

ingredients	Metric	Imperial	American
White fish fillet	450 g	1 lb	1 lb
Natural (plain) yoghurt	150 ml	¼ pt	⅔ cup
Lemon juice	15 ml	1 tbsp	1 tbsp
Cumin, ground	5 ml	1 tsp	1 tsp
Ground coriander (cilantro)	5 ml	1 tsp	1 tsp
Chilli (chili) powder	2.5 ml	½ tsp	½ tsp
Turmeric	2.5 ml	½ tsp	½ tsp
Salt			
Long-grain rice	175 g	6 oz	¾ cup
Can chopped tomatoes	400 g	14 oz	14 oz
Water	300 ml	½ pt	1¼ cups
Chopped coriander, (cilantro) leaves	15 ml	1 tbsp	1 tbsp
To garnish:			
Lemon wedges			
Coriander (cilantro) leaves			

method

1. Cut fish into 4 equal pieces, discarding skin and any bones. Lay in a shallow ovenproof dish, just large enough to take fish in a single layer.

2. Mix yoghurt, lemon juice, spices and a good pinch of salt together. Spoon over fish and turn fish in the mixture to coat completely.

3. If time, leave to marinate for up to 3 hours. If not, cook immediately in a moderate oven, 180°C/350°F/gas mark 4 for 20 minutes, basting occasionally.

4. Meanwhile, put rice in a pan with the tomatoes and water. Bring to the boil, cover, reduce heat and simmer for 20 minutes until cooked and rice

has absorbed the liquid. Add fresh coriander and fork through.

5. Serve fish with the rice, garnished with lemon wedges and fresh coriander leaves.

⏰ Prep time: 10 minutes, plus marinading if time
Cook time: 20 minutes

TROUT IN SOURED CREAM

Use natural (plain) yoghurt instead of cream if you prefer.

serves 4

ingredients	Metric	Imperial	American
Trout, cleaned	4	4	4
Salt and pepper			
Butter	15 g	½ oz	1 tbsp
Oil	15 ml	1 tbsp	1 tbsp
Soured (dairy sour) cream	150 ml	¼ pt	⅔ cup
Chopped (snipped) chives	15 ml	1 tbsp	1 tbsp
Chopped parsley	15 ml	1 tbsp	1 tbsp
To garnish:			
Toasted flaked almonds			
To serve:			
New potatoes			
Baby carrots			

method

1. Rinse fish under running water. Pat dry on kitchen paper. Season and remove heads if liked.

2. Heat butter and oil in a large frying pan (skillet) and fry (sauté) fish for 3 minutes on each side to brown.

3. Add soured cream, herbs and a little more seasoning, if liked. Cover with foil or a lid and simmer for 6 - 8 minutes until fish is cooked through.

4. Transfer fish to warmed serving plates. Stir juices and cream together well and spoon over. Sprinkle with toasted almonds and serve hot with new potatoes and baby carrots.

Prep time: 5 minutes
Cook time: 12 - 20 minutes

WHITING WITH CHEESE AND ANCHOVIES

serves 4

ingredients

	Metric	Imperial	American
Whiting fillets	4	4	4
Butter or margarine	15 g	½ oz	1 tbsp
Oil	10 ml	2 tsp	2 tsp
Tomatoes, sliced	2	2	2
Gruyère or Emmental cheese slices	4	4	4
Canned anchovy fillets, drained	8	8	8
To garnish: Watercress			
To serve: Buttered noodles Mushrooms			

method

1. Skin fillets and remove any bones.
2. Heat butter and oil in a large frying pan (skillet). Add fish and fry (sauté) for 2 minutes.
3. Top with tomato slices, then cheese, then anchovy fillets in a cross on top of each fish fillet.
4. Cover with a lid or foil and cook for 5 - 8 minutes until fish is cooked, and cheese has melted.
5. Transfer to warm serving plates. Garnish with watercress and serve with buttered noodles and mushrooms.

Prep time: 5 minutes
Cook time: 7 - 10 minutes

Beef

Apart from mince for quick-cooking you need to use the more expensive cuts. But the saving on fuel and the lack of waste make them a better buy than you would think... And they taste fantastic!

BEEF AND NOODLE STIR-FRY

serves 4

ingredients	Metric	Imperial	American
Quick-cook Chinese egg noodles	100 g	4 oz	1 cup
Fillet or tenderised minute steak	225 g	8 oz	½ lb
Oil	30 ml	2 tbsp	2 tbsp
Onion, sliced	1	1	1
Carrot, cut into matchsticks	1	1	1
Celery stick (rib), cut into matchsticks	1	1	1
Red (bell) pepper, cut into strips	½	½	½
Mushrooms, sliced	50 g	2 oz	1 cup
Cucumber, cut into matchsticks	¼	¼	¼
Sherry	30 ml	2 tbsp	2 tbsp
Soy sauce	30 ml	2 tbsp	2 tbsp
Demerara (light brown) sugar	15 ml	1 tbsp	1 tbsp
Ground ginger	5 ml	1 tsp	1 tsp
Salt and pepper			

method

1. Cook noodles according to packet directions. Drain.
2. Cut steak diagonally into thin strips.
3. Heat oil in a large pan or wok. Add steak and fry (sauté) for 2 minutes, stirring.
4. Add onion, carrot and celery and continue frying, for a further 3 minutes.
5. Add pepper, mushrooms and cucumber and continue cooking, stirring for 2 minutes.
6. Add noodles and remaining ingredients. Toss well until heated through. Serve straight away.

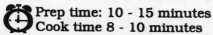
Prep time: 10 - 15 minutes
Cook time 8 - 10 minutes

BURGUNDY-STYLE STEAK

serves 4

ingredients	Metric	Imperial	American
Butter	25 g	1 oz	2 tbsp
Olive oil	30 ml	2 tbsp	2 tbsp
Onion, sliced	1	1	1
Button mushrooms	100 g	4 oz	2 cups
Streaky bacon rashers (slices), diced	2	2	2
Fillet or rump steak, cubed	450 g	1 lb	1 lb
Cornflour (cornstarch)	15 ml	1 tbsp	1 tbsp
Mixed dried herbs	2.5 ml	½ tsp	½ tsp
Brandy	15 ml	1 tbsp	1 tbsp
Red wine	150 ml	¼ pt	⅔ cup
Beef stock	150 ml	¼ pt	⅔ cup
Salt and pepper			
To serve:			
Plain boiled rice			
French beans			

method

1. Melt half the butter and oil in a pan. Add onion, mushrooms and bacon and fry (sauté) for 3 minutes until soft and lightly brown. Remove from pan with a draining spoon.

2. Toss meat in the cornflour and herbs.

3. Heat remaining butter and oil in pan and fry meat quickly for about 5 minutes until browned and cooked through.

4. Add brandy and set alight. When flames subside, add mushroom mixture, wine and stock. Bring to the boil, stirring continually. Season to taste.

5. Serve with rice and green beans.

Prep time: 5 - 10 minutes
Cook time: 8 - 10 minutes

Fillet Steaks Wyrardisbury

serves 4

ingredients

	Metric	Imperial	American
Thin slices French stick	4	4	4
Butter	40 g	1½ oz	3 tbsp
Smooth liver pâté	50 g	2 oz	¼ cup
Fillet steaks	4	4	4
Red wine	90 ml	6 tbsp	6 tbsp
Tomato purée (paste)	15 ml	1 tbsp	1 tbsp
Caster (superfine) sugar	2.5 ml	½ tsp	½ tsp
Dried marjoram	2.5 ml	½ tsp	½ tsp
Salt and pepper			
To garnish:			
Parsley sprigs			
To serve:			
Sautéed potatoes			
Green salad			

method

1. Spread bread on both sides with a little of the butter. Fry (sauté) until golden on each side. Spread with pâté and set aside.

2. Melt remaining butter and fry steaks for 2 - 3 minutes on each side for rare, 5 - 6 minutes each side for well done (depending on thickness).

3. Place a steak on each slice of bread and pâté on warm serving plates and keep warm.

4. Stir wine, tomato purée, marjoram and sugar together in a pan. Bring to the boil stirring and season to taste.

5. Spoon sauce over steaks. Garnish with parsley sprigs and serve with sautéed potatoes and a green salad.

Prep time: 5 minutes
Cook time: up to 15 minutes

MINUTE STEAK DIANE

serves 4

ingredients	Metric	Imperial	American
Minute steaks, tenderised	4	4	4
Lemon juice	10 ml	2 tbsp	2 tbsp
Butter	25 g	1 oz	2 tbsp
Oil	15 ml	1 tbsp	1 tbsp
Small onion, grated	½	½	½
Parsley, chopped	10 ml	2 tsp	2 tsp
Worcestershire sauce	30 ml	2 tbsp	2 tbsp
To garnish:			
Cherry tomatoes, sliced			
To serve:			
Puréed potatoes			
Broccoli spears			

method

1. Brush surfaces of the steaks with lemon juice.
2. Heat butter and oil in a frying pan (skillet) and fry (sauté) steaks for 2 - 3 minutes on each side until cooked through (do not attempt to cook them rare). Transfer to warm serving plates. Keep warm.
3. Add onion, parsley and Worcestershire sauce to pan juices. Cook gently for one minute then spoon over steaks.
4. Garnish with sliced cherry tomatoes and serve with puréed potatoes and broccoli.

note:

For a cheaper alternative, use vey thin slices of top rump, well beaten with a rolling pin or meat tenderiser.

Prep time: 5 minutes
Cook time: 5 - 7 minutes

Pasta Grill

serves 4

ingredients

	Metric	Imperial	American
Pasta shapes	225 g	8 oz	2 cups
Onion, chopped	1	1	1
Garlic clove, crushed	1	1	1
Minced (ground) beef	225 g	8 oz	1 cup
Can tomatoes	400 g	14 oz	14 oz
Mixed dried herbs	2.5 ml	½ tsp	½ tsp
Salt and pepper			
Cheddar cheese, grated	75 g	3 oz	¾ cup
To serve:			
Mixed salad			

method

1. Cook pasta according to packet directions, drain.
2. Meanwhile, fry (sauté) onion, garlic and beef in a pan and stir until browned and meat grains are separate.
3. Add tomatoes, break up with a wooden spoon. Stir in herbs and a little salt and pepper. Bring to the boil, reduce heat and simmer for 10 minutes until cooked through and sauce is reduced.
4. Stir in pasta. Turn into a 1.5L/2¼ pt/6 cups flameproof dish. Sprinkle with cheese and place under a hot grill (broiler) until cheese is melted and golden.
5. Serve hot with a mixed salad.

Prep time: 5 minutes
Cook time: 15 minutes

PIED-À-TERRE PIE

serves 4

ingredients	Metric	Imperial	American
Onion, finely chopped	1	1	1
Minced (ground) beef	450 g	1 lb	2 cups
Plain (all-purpose) flour	15 ml	1 tbsp	1 tbsp
Beef stock	300 ml	½ pt	1¼ cups
Frozen peas	75 g	3 oz	¾ cup
Gravy salt or browning			
Salt and pepper			
Potatoes, thinly sliced	450 g	1 lb	1 lb
Cheddar cheese, grated	75 g	3 oz	¾ cup
To serve:			
Carrots			

method

1. Fry (sauté) onion and beef in a pan until meat is browned and onion is softened. Stir to break up meat.
2. Add flour and cook for one minute.
3. Pour in stock, gravy salt or browning and add peas. Bring to the boil, stirring. Reduce heat and simmer for 10 minutes.
4. Meanwhile cook sliced potatoes in boiling salted water for about 4 minutes until cooked. Drain.
5. Taste and season meat mixture, then turn into a 1.5 L/2½ pt/6 cups flameproof dish.
6. Top with sliced potatoes then sprinkle with grated cheese. Place under a hot grill (broiler) until golden brown. Serve with carrots.

Prep time: 10 minutes
Cook time: about 20 minutes

POPOVERS

A great way to use up left over roast beef or other joints, and vegetables on Monday.

makes 8

ingredients	Metric	Imperial	American
Oil			
Plain (all-purpose) flour	50 g	2 oz	½ cup
Salt	pinch	pinch	pinch
Eggs	1	1	1
Milk	75 ml	5 tbsp	5 tbsp
Water	75 ml	5 tbsp	5 tbsp
Roast beef, cut in small dice	45 ml	3 tbsp	3 tbsp
Cooked, leftover vegetables, chopped	45 ml	3 tbsp	3 tbsp
To serve:			
Gravy and a green vegetable			

method

1. Put 5 ml/1 tsp oil into each of eight sections of a bun tin (muffin pan). Place in a hot oven, 230°C/450°F/gas mark 8.
2. Put flour and salt in a bowl. Add egg and half the milk and water and beat until smooth. Stir in remaining milk and water.
3. Divide meat and vegetables between tins. Spoon batter over and cook towards the top of the oven for 15 - 18 minutes until puffy and golden.
4. Serve hot with gravy and a green vegetable.

Prep time: 5 - 10 minutes
Cook time: 15 - 18 minutes

QUICK CHILLI

Serve with cornmeal pancakes (see p. 172) instead of rice if you prefer

serves 4

ingredients	Metric	Imperial	American
Onion, chopped	1	1	1
Garlic clove, crushed	1	1	1
Minced (ground) beef	350 g	12 oz	1½ cups
Hot chilli (chili) powder	2.5 ml	½ tsp	½ tsp
Ground cumin	5 ml	1 tsp	1 tsp
Dried oregano	5 ml	1 tsp	1 tsp
Can tomatoes	400 g	14 oz	14 oz
Can red kidney beans, drained	425 g	15 oz	15 oz
Tomato purée (paste)	15 ml	1 tbsp	1 tbsp
Salt and pepper			
To serve:			
Plain boiled rice			
Cheddar cheese, grated			
Shredded lettuce			

method

1. Put onion, garlic and beef in a pan and fry (sauté) until browned and grains of meat are separate.

2. Add chilli powder and cumin and fry for one minute more.

3. Stir in herbs and tomatoes and break up with a wooden spoon, then add beans, tomato purée and seasoning to taste.

4. Bring to the boil, reduce heat and simmer for 10 - 15 minutes until reduced and a good rich colour.

5. Serve with plain boiled rice, with grated cheese and lettuce shredded to sprinkle over.

Prep time: 5 minutes
Cook time: 15 - 20 minutes

SALT BEEF AND POTATO SALAD

This salad is also good with cubes of boiled gammon.

serves 4 - 6

ingredients	Metric	Imperial	American
Cooked salt beef, cubed	175 g	6 oz	good 1 cup
Cold potatoes, cut in chunks	750 g	1½ lb	1½ lb
Small red (bell) pepper, diced	1	1	1
Cucumber, diced	¼	¼	¼
Can sweetcorn, (corn) drained	198 g	7 oz	7 oz
Olive oil	60 ml	4 tbsp	4 tbsp
Wine vinegar	30 ml	2 tbsp	2 tbsp
Dijon mustard	2.5 ml	½ tsp	½ tsp
Caster (superfine) sugar	2.5 ml	½ tsp	½ tsp
Salt and pepper			
To garnish:			
Onion rings			

method

1. Put meat and vegetables in a large salad bowl.
2. Blend oil, vinegar, mustard, sugar and a little salt and pepper together and pour over the meat and vegetables. Toss well.
3. Garnish with onion rings and serve.

Prep time: 10 minutes

TRIPE ROMANOV

serves 4

ingredients

	Metric	Imperial	American
Blanched ox tripe	450 g	1 lb	1 lb
Red wine vinegar	30 ml	2 tbsp	2 tbsp
Olive oil	30 ml	2 tbsp	2 tbsp
Butter	50 g	2 oz	¼ cup
Mushrooms, sliced	100 g	4 oz	2 cups
Leek, sliced	1	1	1
Plain (all-purpose) flour	25 g	1 oz	¼ cup
Can chopped tomatoes	400 g	14 oz	14 oz
Salt and pepper			
Fresh breadcrumbs	50 g	2 oz	1 cup
To serve:			
Peas and crusty bread			

method

1. Cut tripe into thin strips. Toss in the vinegar and oil.

2. Melt 40 g/1½ oz/3 tbsp of the butter in a pan and fry (sauté) mushrooms and leek stirring for one minute. Cover and cook gently for a further 3 - 4 minutes until soft.

3. Stir in the flour, tomatoes and tripe. Bring to the boil and simmer for 5 minutes, stirring. Season.

4. Turn into a greased ovenproof dish. Top with breadcrumbs and dot with butter.

5. Bake in a hot oven 220°C/425°F/gas mark 7 for about 20 minutes until cooked through and topping is golden.

6. Serve with peas and crusty bread.

Prep time: 5 - 10 minutes
Cook time: 30 minutes

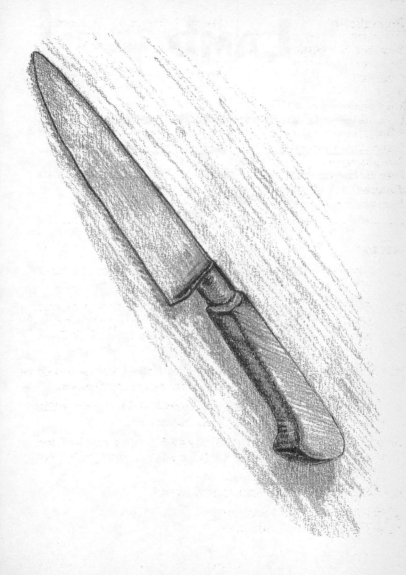

Lamb

One of the most versatile of meats, Lamb lends itself to dishes from all over the world.

Eastern Lamb

A great way of using up the left-over Sunday joint. Use any leftover vegetables and gravy with a little tomato purée (paste) and curry powder to taste, to make a curry accompaniment.

serves 4

ingredients	Metric	Imperial	American
Onion, sliced	1	1	1
Oil	15 ml	1 tbsp	1 tbsp
Cooked lamb, diced	225 g	8 oz	good 1½ cups
Garlic clove, crushed	1	1	1
Ground ginger	2.5 ml	½ tsp	½ tsp
Ground cumin	2.5 ml	½ tsp	½ tsp
Ground coriander (cilantro)	2.5 ml	½ tsp	½ tsp
Turmeric	7.5 ml	1½ tsp	1½ tsp
Natural (plain) yoghurt	150 ml	¼ pt	⅔ cup
Salt and pepper			
To garnish:			
Desiccated (shredded) coconut			
Currants			
To serve:			
Pilau rice			

method

1. Fry (sauté) the onion in oil for 3 minutes until turning golden.
2. Add lamb and remaining ingredients. Simmer for about 20 minutes, stirring occasionally until almost dry (the mixture will curdle and look watery at first).
3. Serve on a bed of pilau rice, with desiccated coconut and currants sprinkled over.

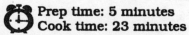
Prep time: 5 minutes
Cook time: 23 minutes

Greek-Style Lamb Kebabs

These kebabs are equally delicious prepared with cubes of pork fillet.

serves 4

ingredients	Metric	Imperial	American
Lamb neck fillet	350 g	12 oz	¾ lb
Olive oil	15 ml	1 tbsp	1 tbsp
Red wine vinegar	10 ml	2 tsp	2 tsp
Dried oregano	5 ml	1 tsp	1 tsp
Salt and pepper			
Green (bell) pepper	½	½	½
Button mushrooms	8	8	8
To serve:			
Buttered rice			
Mixed salad with olives and Feta cheese			

method

1. Cut meat into cubes. Put in a bowl.
2. Drizzle with oil, vinegar, herbs and seasoning. Toss and leave for at least 10 minutes (longer if possible).
3. Cut pepper into 8 pieces. Thread meat onto 4 skewers, alternating with mushrooms and pepper pieces.
4. Grill (broil) until golden and cooked through, about 10 minutes turning once or twice and brushing with any left over marinade.
5. Serve hot with buttered rice and a mixed salad topped with olives and Feta cheese.

Prep time: 20 minutes, including marinating
Cook time: 10 minutes

LEMON GLAZED CUTLETS

Try this with other citrus fruit too. For larger appetites, double the ingredients.

serves 4

ingredients	Metric	Imperial	American
Lamb cutlets	4	4	4
Seasoned plain (all-purpose) flour	15 g	1 tbsp	1 tbsp
Butter	25 g	1 oz	2 tbsp
Lemon, grated rind and juice	1	1	1
Caster (superfine) sugar	10 ml	2 tsp	2 tsp
To garnish:			
Parsley			
To serve:			
Buttered noodles			
Matchstick carrots			

method

1. Coat lamb cutlets in seasoned flour, tapping off excess.

2. Fry (sauté) in butter for about 10 minutes until browned and cooked through, turning once.

3. Remove and keep warm.

4. Drain off all but 15 ml/1 tbsp of fat from pan. Add lemon juice and rind and sugar and heat through. Spoon over cutlets, garnish with parsley and serve immediately with buttered noodles and matchstick carrots.

Prep time: 5 minutes
Cook time: 12 minutes

Liver with Bacon and Onion Sauce

For larger appetites, cook more slices of liver.

serves 4

ingredients	Metric	Imperial	American
Bacon rashers (slices)	8	8	8
Oil	15 ml	1 tbsp	1 tbsp
Lamb's liver slices	4	4	4
Onions, roughly chopped	3	3	3
Water	150 ml	¼ pt	⅔ cup
Plain (all-purpose) flour	20 g	¾ oz	1½ tbsp
Milk	150 ml	¼ pt	⅔ cup
Salt and pepper			
To garnish:			
Chopped parsley			
To serve:			
Plain boiled potatoes			
A green vegetable			

method

1. Dry-fry bacon until browned on both sides in a frying pan (skillet). Transfer to a serving dish and keep warm.

2. Heat oil in the same pan and fry (sauté) liver for about 4 minutes, turning once until browned and just cooked.

3. Meanwhile, boil onions in the water for 4 minutes in a covered pan. Blend flour and milk, add to pan and boil for 2 minutes, stirring. Season to taste.

4. Garnish liver and bacon with parsley and serve with the onion sauce, boiled potatoes and a green vegetable.

Prep time: 5 minutes
Cook time: about 10 minutes

Quick Moussaka

Use minced (ground) beef instead of lamb if you prefer.

serves 4

ingredients	Metric	Imperial	American
Onion, finely chopped	1	1	1
Garlic clove, crushed	1	1	1
Minced (ground) lamb	350 g	12 oz	1½ cups
Aubergine (eggplant), sliced	1	1	1
Lamb or chicken stock	150 ml	¼ pt	⅔ cup
Tomato purée (paste)	30 ml	2 tbsp	2 tbsp
Ground cinnamon	5 ml	1 tsp	1 tsp
Dried oregano	2.5 ml	½ tsp	½ tsp
Salt and pepper			
Natural (plain) yoghurt	150 ml	¼ pt	⅔ cup
Egg	1	1	1
Cheddar cheese, grated	75 g	3 oz	¾ cup
To serve:			
Herby Pittas (p.174)			
Green salad			

method

1. Fry (sauté) onion, garlic and mince together in a saucepan, stirring until grains of meat are brown and separate.
2. Add stock and boil for about 5 minutes until nearly all the liquid has evaporated.
3. Stir in tomato purée, cinnamon, and oregano. Season to taste and simmer for 5 minutes.
4. Meanwhile, boil aubergine in salted water for about 5 minutes or until tender. Drain.
5. Layer meat mixture and aubergine in a 1.5 litre/2½ pt/6 cups flameproof dish, finishing with a layer of aubergine.
6. Beat yoghurt, egg and cheese together, spoon over. Place under a moderately hot grill (broiler) until

topping is set and golden, about 5 minutes.
7. Serve with Herby Pittas and a green salad.

Prep time: 10 minutes
Cook time: about 20 minutes

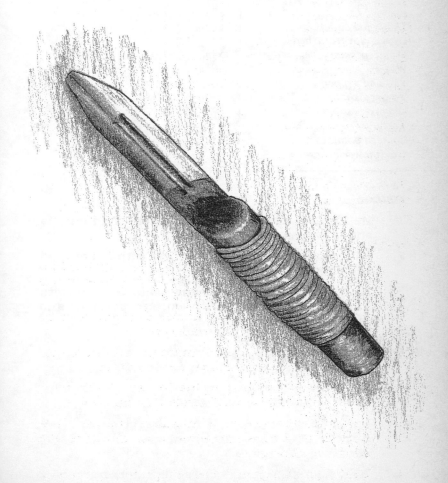

ROSIE'S CUTLETS

Try this dish with leg of lamb steaks too, but remember they'll take a little longer to cook.

serves 4

ingredients	Metric	Imperial	American
Butter	25 g	1 oz	2 tbsp
Thin lamb cutlets	8	8	8
Garlic clove, crushed	1	1	1
Dried rosemary, crushed	5 ml	1 tsp	1 tsp
Water	60 ml	4 tbsp	4 tbsp
Salt and pepper			
To garnish:			
Watercress			
To serve:			
Sautéed potatoes			
Cauliflower cheese			

method

1. Melt butter in a frying pan (skillet). Add cutlets and brown on both sides.

2. Add remaining ingredients, cover with foil or a lid and simmer for 10 minutes.

3. Transfer to a warmed serving dish. Garnish with watercress and serve with sautéed potatoes and cauliflower cheese.

Prep time: 5 minutes
Cook time: 12 minutes

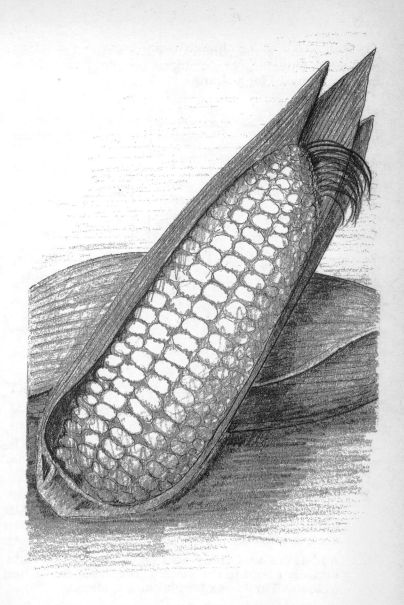

SAUCY LAMB WITH CAPERS

Another great recipe which uses leftovers. Try using courgettes (zucchini) or aubergine (eggplant) instead of marrow (squash) for a change.

serves 4

ingredients

	Metric	Imperial	American
Butter or margarine	75 g	3 oz	1/3 cup
Slices of bread, cubed	3	3	3
Marrow (squash), peeled and diced	350 g	12 oz	2¼ cups
Mushrooms, quartered	100 g	4 oz	2 cups
Cooked lamb, diced	175 g	6 oz	good 1 cup
Plain (all-purpose) flour	15 ml	1 tbsp	1 tbsp
Chicken or lamb stock	300 ml	½ pt	1¼ cups
Capers, chopped	15 ml	1 tbsp	1 tbsp
Chopped parsley	15 ml	1 tbsp	1 tbsp
Egg, beaten	1	1	1
Salt and pepper			
To serve:			
Shredded cabbage in vinaigrette			

method

1. Melt 50 g/2 oz/¼ cup of the butter or margarine in a pan. Toss bread in it to coat then remove from pan and set aside.

2. Melt remaining fat in pan. Add marrow and mushrooms. Cover and cook gently for 5-10 minutes until vegetables are tender, shaking pan occasionally.

3. Add lamb and flour and cook stirring for one minute. Blend in the stock and add capers. Bring to the boil and cook for 2 minutes, stirring.

4. Blend in parsley and egg and season to taste.

5. Spoon into 4 fireproof individual dishes. Top with bread and place under a hot grill (broiler) until bread is browned. Serve hot with shredded cabbage in vinaigrette.

Prep time: 10 minutes
Cook time: 10 - 15 minutes

SOMERSET LAMB

serves 4

ingredients	Metric	Imperial	American
Onion, thinly sliced	1	1	1
Cooking (tart) apple, sliced	1	1	1
Oil	15 ml	1 tbsp	1 tbsp
Lamb chump chops	4	4	4
Plain (all-purpose) flour	20 g	¾ oz	1½ tbsp
Cider or apple juice	300 ml	½ pt	1¼ cups
Chopped mint	15ml	1 tbsp	1 tbsp
To garnish:			
Mint sprigs			
To serve:			
Jacket potatoes			
Spring greens			

method

1. Fry (sauté) onion and apple in the oil for 3-4 minutes until softened. Remove from pan.

2. Trim any excess fat from chops. Fry for about 10 - 15 minutes, turning once, until just cooked through.

2. Transfer onion, apple and chops to a warmed serving dish, keep warm.

3. Blend flour with a little of the cider or apple juice. Stir in remainder of juice and pour into pan. Add mint, bring to the boil and cook for 2 minutes, stirring. Season to taste.

4. Spoon sauce over lamb, garnish with sprigs of mint and serve with jacket potatoes and spring greens.

Prep time: 10 minutes
Cook time: 15 - 20 minutes

TIDDLEY KIDNEYS

serves 4

ingredients	Metric	Imperial	American
Butter or margarine	25 g	1 oz	2 tbsp
Lamb's kidneys, cored and quartered	8	8	8
Mushrooms, sliced	100 g	4 oz	2 cups
Onions, sliced	2	2	2
Single (light) cream	45 ml	3 tbsp	3 tbsp
Sherry	15 ml	1 tbsp	1 tbsp
Salt and pepper			
To garnish:			
Chopped parsley			
To serve:			
Creamed potatoes			
Leaf spinach			

method

1. Melt fat in a frying pan (skillet).
2. Add kidneys, mushrooms and onions. Cover with foil or a lid and cook, stirring occasionally, for 10 minutes.
3. Add cream, sherry and seasoning. Heat through.
4. Spoon into a nest of creamed potatoes, sprinkle with chopped parsley and serve with leaf spinach.

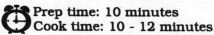
Prep time: 10 minutes
Cook time: 10 - 12 minutes

Pork

Pork is one of the richest and most flavoursome of meats. The danger is cooking it to death when it becomes dry and stringy. All these dishes will give you succulent, tender results. But don't keep prodding it with a fork as it cooks or all the juice will run out.

AUSTRIAN PORK CHOPS

serves 4

ingredients	Metric	Imperial	American
Boneless thin pork chops	4	4	4
Olive oil	15 ml	1 tbsp	1 tbsp
Onion, thinly sliced	1	1	1
Garlic clove, crushed	1	1	1
Small cabbage, shredded	½	½	½
Vegetable or pork stock	150 ml	¼ pt	⅔ cup
Salt and pepper			
Caraway seeds	15 ml	1 tbsp	1 tbsp
To garnish:			
Chopped parsley			
To serve:			
Boiled potatoes			

method

1. Fry (sauté) chops in the oil in a deep frying pan (skillet) for 3 minutes on each side to brown. Remove from pan.

2. Add onion and garlic and fry for 2 minutes.

3. Stir in the cabbage and cook, stirring, for about 3 minutes until it softens slightly. Add stock.

4. Lay chops on top, sprinkle with the caraway seeds and a little salt and pepper. Cover with foil or a lid, reduce heat and simmer for 20 minutes until tender.

5. Garnish with chopped parsley and serve with plain boiled potatoes.

Prep time: 10 minutes
Cook time: about 30 minutes

BACON EGG AND AVOCADO SALAD

Cold, soft poached eggs are magnificent in this salad. But the less adventurous may prefer to cook the eggs for longer.

serves 4

ingredients	Metric	Imperial	American
Eggs	4	4	4
Lemon juice	10ml	2 tsp	2 tsp
Streaky bacon rashers (slices)	4	4	4
Avocados	2	2	2
Mixed salad greens (including radiccio or Lollo Rosso)	225g	8 oz	8 oz
Olive oil	30ml	2 tbsp	2 tbsp
Wine vinegar	10ml	2 tsp	2 tsp
Salt and pepper			
To garnish:			
Onion rings			
Croûtons			
To serve:			
Garlic bread (p. 173) or Hot Herb Loaf (p.174)			

method

1. Poach eggs in gently simmering water to which half the lemon juice has been added. Poach for about 3 minutes until whites are set but yolk is still soft (or longer if you like them hard).

2. Carefully lift out with a draining spoon and place them in a bowl of cold water to prevent cooking any further.

3. Grill (broil) or dry-fry bacon rashers until crisp. Cut into pieces with scissors.

4. Halve, peel and slice avocados, discarding stones (pits). Toss in remaining lemon juice.

5. Put salad greens in a bowl, add avocado and bacon and toss in the oil, vinegar and a little salt and pepper. Transfer to 4 individual serving bowls.

6. Lift eggs out of water with a draining spoon and put one in each bowl. Garnish with the onion rings and croûtons and serve with garlic or herb bread.

Prep time: 10 minutes
Cook time: about 6 minutes

Barbecued Pork

serves 4

ingredients	Metric	Imperial	American
Butter or margarine	15 g	½ oz	1 tbsp
Pork shoulder steaks	4	4	4
Lemon juice	15 ml	1 tbsp	1 tbsp
Malt vinegar	15 ml	1 tbsp	1 tbsp
Tomato purée (paste)	30 ml	2 tbsp	2 tbsp
Worcestershire sauce	15 ml	1 tbsp	1 tbsp
Golden (light corn) syrup	30 ml	2 tbsp	2 tbsp
To serve:			
Savoury rice			
Watercress and beansprout salad			

method

1. Melt fat in a large frying pan (skillet). Add pork and fry (sauté) for 3 minutes on each side to brown.

2. Blend remaining ingredients together. Spoon over pork. Cook over a moderate heat for about 10 minutes turning meat occasionally, until pork is coated in a sticky glaze.

3. Serve on a bed of savoury rice with a watercress and beansprout salad.

Prep time: 5 minutes
Cook time: 16 minutes

Broccoli and Ham au Gratin

Omit the ham to turn this into a delicious accompaniment for plain grills or a vegetarian lunch dish (if you use vegetarian cheese).

serves 4

ingredients

ingredients	Metric	Imperial	American
Broccoli	450 g	1 lb	1 lb
Ham slices	4	4	4
Plain (all purpose) flour	25 g	1 oz	1/4 cup
Butter or margarine	25 g	1 oz	2 tbsp
Milk	300 g	1/2 pt	1 1/4 cups
Cheddar cheese, grated	100 g	4 oz	1 cup
Salt and pepper			
To serve:			
Crusty bread			

method

1. Separate broccoli into florets and cook in boiling salted water for about 5 minutes until tender.

2. Divide into 8 bundles and wrap half a slice of ham around each.

3. Lay side-by-side in a buttered ovenproof dish.

4. Whisk flour and fat into milk in a pan. Bring to the boil and boil for 2 minutes, whisking all the time until thickened and smooth. Stir in 75 g/3 oz/¾ cup of the cheese and season to taste.

5. Pour the sauce over the broccoli and ham. Sprinkle with remaining cheese and grill (broil) for about 4 minutes until golden brown. Serve with crusty bread.

Prep time: 10 minutes
Cook time: 10 minutes

DELUXE GRILL

serves 4

ingredients

	Metric	Imperial	American
Gammon steaks	4	4	4
Can pineapple chunks	200 g	7 oz	7 oz
Tomatoes, skinned and chopped	4	4	4
Havarti, Gruyère or Emmental cheese slices	4	4	4
To garnish:			
Watercress			
To serve:			
Sautéed potatoes			
Green beans			

method

1. Snip edges of gammon with scissors to prevent curling.
2. Drain and roughly chop pineapple and mix with tomatoes.
3. Grill (broil) gammon for 5 minutes on each side.
4. Spread fruit over and top each with a slice of cheese.
5. Return to the grill (broiler) until cheese has melted and fruit is hot.
6. Garnish with watercress and serve with sautéed potatoes and green beans.

Prep time: 10 minutes
Cook time: about 15 minutes

DEVILLED KIDNEYS

You can use lamb's kidneys instead, in which case use 8 for four people.

serves 4

ingredients	Metric	Imperial	American
Pig's kidneys	4	4	4
Streaky bacon rashers (slices)	4	4	4
Butter or margarine	50 g	2 oz	4 tbsp
Mild curry powder	5 ml	1 tsp	1 tsp
English mustard, made	2.5 ml	½ tsp	½ tsp
Worcestershire sauce	10 ml	2 tsp	2 tsp
Tomato ketchup (catsup)	30 ml	2 tbsp	2 tbsp
Salt and pepper			
To garnish:			
Chopped parsley			
To serve:			
Boiled rice			
Courgettes (zucchini)			

method

1. Cut kidneys into bite-sized pieces, discarding cores. Dice bacon.

2. Melt butter in a frying pan (skillet) and fry (sauté) kidneys and bacon over a moderate heat for 3 minutes, stirring.

3. Add remaining ingredients, mix well and cook, stirring for about 5 - 8 minutes until kidneys are cooked, but still tender and bathed in sauce.

4. Garnish with parsley. Serve with rice and courgettes.

Prep time: 5 minutes
Cook time: 8 - 11 minutes

FEGATTINI

Use ripe tomatoes for the sauce for these meatballs.

serves 4

ingredients	Metric	Imperial	American
Pig's liver	350 g	12 oz	¾ lb
Onions	2	2	2
Slice of bread	1	1	1
Chopped sage	15 ml	1 tbsp	1 tbsp
Egg, beaten	1	1	1
Salt and pepper			
Olive oil	15 ml	1 tbsp	1 tbsp
Tomatoes, quartered	450 g	1 lb	1 lb
Tomato purée (paste)	15 ml	1 tbsp	1 tbsp
Water	60 ml	4 tbsp	4 tbsp
Sugar	2.5 ml	½ tsp	½ tsp
To serve:			
Tagliatelle			
Green salad			

method

1. Coarsely mince (grind) or process liver, one onion and the bread. Add sage, egg, seasoning and tomatoes and mix well.

2. Chop remaining onion. Soften in oil for 2 minutes. Add tomato purée and water, cover and cook for about 5 minutes, stirring occasionally until pulpy. Season and add sugar.

3. Meanwhile bring a large pan of salted water to the boil. Drop in tablespoons of the liver mixture and simmer for about 4 minutes until cooked through. Drain.

4. Put cooked, balls of liver mixture in the sauce, heat through and serve with tagliatelle and a green salad.

Prep time: 10 minutes
Cook time: about 10 minutes in all.

ORIENTAL PORK SLICES

serves 4

ingredients	Metric	Imperial	American
Belly pork slices	8	8	8
Cornflour (cornstarch)	10 ml	2 tsp	2 tsp
Vinegar	15 ml	1 tbsp	1 tbsp
Can crushed pineapple	250 g	9 oz	9 oz
Tomato ketchup (catsup)	30 ml	2 tbsp	2 tbsp
Soy sauce	15 ml	1 tbsp	1 tbsp
Cucumber, diced	1/4	1/4	1/4
To serve:			
Boiled rice			
Green (bell) pepper and grated carrot salad			

method

1. Discard any rind or bones in pork, then fry (sauté) slices over a moderate heat for about 15 - 20 minutes, turning once or twice until browned and cooked through.

2. Meanwhile blend cornflour with the vinegar in a pan.

3. Add remaining ingredients. Bring to the boil, stirring and simmer for 5 minutes, stirring occasionally.

4. Spoon over pork and serve with boiled rice and a green pepper and grated carrot salad.

Prep time: 5 minutes
Cook time: 20 - 25 minutes

PORK STROGANOFF

This recipe is also good made with chicken breasts or fillet steak.

serves 4

ingredients	Metric	Imperial	American
Pork fillet	350 g	12 oz	¾ lb
Butter or margarine	25 g	1 oz	2 tbsp
Onion, sliced	1	1	1
Mushrooms, sliced	100 g	4 oz	2 cups
Brandy	15 ml	1 tbsp	1 tbsp
Soured (dairy sour) cream	150 ml	¼ pt	⅔ cup
Salt and pepper			
To garnish:			
Chopped parsley			
To serve:			
Buttered rice			
Green salad			

method

1. Cut pork into thin strips.
2. Melt butter and fry (sauté) onion and mushrooms for 3 minutes to soften.
3. Add pork strips and fry for 5 - 8 minutes until cooked through.
4. Put brandy in a soup ladle, set alight then pour into pan. Cook until flames subside. Stir in cream and heat through but do not boil.
5. Season to taste. Garnish with chopped parsley and serve with buttered rice and a green salad.

Prep time: 10 minutes
Cook time: 10 - 12 minutes

Spaghetti with Bacon and Eggs

Use less or more spaghetti according to appetites.

serves 4

ingredients	Metric	Imperial	American
Onion, finely chopped	1	1	1
Garlic clove, crushed	2	2	2
Streaky bacon rashers (slices), diced	6	6	6
Olive oil	60 ml	4 tbsp	4 tbsp
Spaghetti	350 g	12 oz	¾ lb
Chopped parsley	15 ml	1 tbsp	1 tbsp
Eggs	2	2	2
Milk or single (light) cream	30 ml	2 tbsp	2 tbsp
Salt and pepper			
To serve:			
Parmesan cheese, grated			
Salad			

method

1. Fry (sauté) onion, garlic and bacon in the oil for 2 minutes, cover and cook gently for 5 minutes until onion is soft.

2. Meanwhile cook spaghetti according to packet directions, drain and return to pan.

3. Stir in bacon mixture and parsley. Beat eggs with milk or cream. Add to pan. Toss over a gently heat until creamy but do not boil or egg will scramble. Season and serve with grated Parmesan cheese and salad.

Prep time: 5 - 10 minutes
Cook time: about 15 minutes

STICKY ORANGE STEAKS

serves 4

ingredients

	Metric	Imperial	American
Pork or bacon steaks	4	4	4
Butter or margarine	15 g	½ oz	1 tbsp
Orange jelly marmalade	15 ml	1 tbsp	1 tbsp
Ground ginger	2.5 ml	½ tsp	½ tsp
Orange juice	5 ml	1 tsp	1 tsp
To garnish:			
Orange slices			
To serve:			
Buttered noodles			
Mangetout (snow peas)			

method

1. Fry (sauté) steaks on one side for 5 minutes in the butter.
2. Mix marmalade, ginger and orange juice together.
3. Turn steaks over and brush with this mixture.
4. Fry for a further 5 minutes, basting occasionally with the juices.
5. Place pan under a hot grill (broiler) for 2 minutes until glaze is sticky. Transfer steaks to warm serving plates, garnish with orange slices and serve hot with buttered noodles and mangetout.

Prep time: 2 minutes
Cook time: 12 minutes

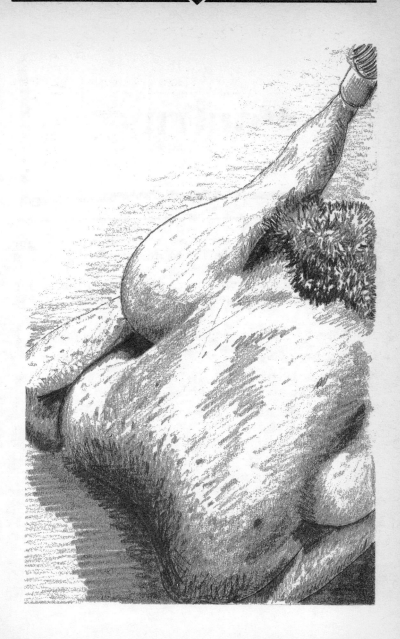

Poultry

Chicken and turkey are always excellent value for money and lend themselves to an infinite number of recipes.

Duck is a more expensive proposition but it has exquisite flavour, well worth treating yourself to.

Cheesy Chicken Topper

serves 4

ingredients

	Metric	Imperial	American
Chicken breast fillets	4	4	4
Butter, melted	20 g	¾ oz	1½ tbsp
Lean ham slices	4	4	4
Gruyère or Cheddar cheese, grated	100 g	4 oz	1 cup
To garnish:			
Tomato wedges			
Watercress			
To serve:			
New potatoes			
Peas			

method

1. Place chicken breasts in a plastic bag one at a time and beat with a rolling pin to flatten.

2. Brush chicken breasts with melted butter and grill (broil) for 3 minutes on each side.

3. Trim ham to fit chicken. Place on top and cover liberally with grated cheese.

4. Grill until cheese is melted and turning golden.

5. Serve garnished with tomato wedges with new potatoes and peas.

Prep time: 10 minutes
Cook time: 8 - 10 minutes

Chicken and Coconut Masala

serves 4

ingredients	Metric	Imperial	American
Boneless chicken meat, diced	350g	12 oz	scant 2½ cups
Onion, chopped	1	1	1
Small green (bell) pepper, sliced	1	1	1
Mild curry powder	15 ml	1 tbsp	1 tbsp
Oil	30 ml	2 tbsp	2 tbsp
Chicken stock	450 ml	¾ pt	2 cups
Packet creamed coconut	½	½	½
Ground almonds	30 ml	2 tbsp	2 tbsp
Raisins	15 ml	1 tbsp	1 tbsp
Salt and pepper			
Chopped coriander (cilantro)	15 ml	1 tbsp	1 tbsp
To garnish:			
Lemon wedges			
To serve:			
Pilau rice			

method

1. Fry (sauté) chicken, onion, pepper and curry powder in the oil for 4 minutes, stirring.

2. Add stock, coconut, ground almonds and raisins. Bring to the boil, reduce heat and simmer for about 10 minutes until chicken is cooked.

3. If sauce is still a little runny, remove chicken with a draining spoon and boil sauce rapidly, stirring, until reduced and thickened.

4. Season to taste. Return chicken to sauce and stir in chopped fresh coriander.

5. Serve on a bed of pilau rice, garnished with lemon wedges.

Prep time: 10 minutes
Cook time: 14 - 20 minutes

Chicken in Filo Pastry

serves 4

ingredients

	Metric	Imperial	American
Boneless chicken breasts	4	4	4
Butter	25 g	1 oz	2 tbsp
Filo pastry sheets	4	4	4
Salt and pepper			
Cranberry sauce	40 ml	8 tsp	8 tsp
Can asparagus spears	300 g	11 oz	11 oz
Single (light) cream	30 ml	2 tbsp	2 tbsp
Grated nutmeg	1.25 ml	¼ tsp	¼ tsp
To garnish:			
Parsley sprigs			
To serve:			
A medley of young vegetables			

method

1. Fry (sauté) chicken breasts in half the butter for 5 minutes, until almost cooked, turning once.
2. Melt remaining butter. Brush a little on pastry sheets and fold in half.
3. Put 10 ml/2 tsp of cranberry sauce in centres of sheets. Top with chicken. Fold pastry over.
4. Transfer, folded side down to a buttered baking sheet and brush with remaining butter.
5. Bake in a hot oven, 200°C/400°F/gas mark 6 for about 15 minutes until golden brown.
6. Meanwhile drain asparagus, reserving liquid and sieve or liquidise. Place in a small pan and add cream. Thin with a little of the reserved liquid, if necessary. Add nutmeg and heat through.
7. Transfer parcels to warmed serving plates. Spoon a little of the sauce to one side and garnish with parsley. Serve with a medley of vegetables.

Prep time: 10 - 15 minutes
Cook time: 20 minutes

CHICKEN HAWAII

You can substitute a can of pineapple chunks in natural juice if you prefer, then serve the salad on a bed of lettuce.

serves 4

ingredients	Metric	Imperial	American
Fresh pineapple	1	1	1
Long-grain rice, cooked	175 g	6 oz	1½ cups
Chicken meat, cooked and diced	175 g	6 oz	good 1 cup
Can sweetcorn (corn) with (bell) peppers, drained	198 g	7 oz	7 oz
Mayonnaise	30 ml	2 tbsp	2 tbsp
Salt and pepper			
To garnish:			
Tomato wedges			
To serve:			
Green salad			

method

1. Cut green top off pineapple about 5cm/2 in down from the stalk. Loosen flesh with a serrated knife. Scoop out into a bowl, leaving shell intact.

2. Roughly chop fruit, discarding any tough core. Drain off excess juice. Place in a bowl.

3. Add rice, sweetcorn and mayonnaise. Mix well and season to taste.

4. Pile mixture back into pineapple shell placed on a serving plate on a bed of lettuce. Put green top back on as a 'lid'. Spoon any mixture that won't fit in shell around edge. Garnish with tomato wedges and serve with a green salad.

Prep time: 15 - 20 minutes

Chinese-Style Chicken with Cashew Nuts

serves 4

ingredients

	Metric	Imperial	American
Boneless chicken thighs	225 g	8 oz	½ lb
Bunch spring onions (scallions)	1	1	1
Oil	30 ml	2 tbsp	2 tbsp
Carrot, grated	1	1	1
Beansprouts	300 g	10 oz	5 cups
Cashew nuts	25 g	1 oz	¼ cup
Chicken stock	300 ml	½ pt	1¼ cups
Cornflour (cornstarch)	15 ml	1 tbsp	1 tbsp
Soy sauce	15 ml	1 tbsp	1 tbsp
To serve:			
Fried rice			

method

1. Cut meat into neat strips.
2. Trim and chop spring onions into 2.5cm/1 in pieces.
3. Heat oil in a wok or large frying pan (skillet). Fry (sauté) chicken, onions and carrot, stirring, for 5 minutes.
4. Add beansprouts and cook, stirring, for 3 minutes.
5. Add cashew nuts and stock.
6. Blend cornflour with soy sauce and stir into pan. Bring to the boil and cook for 2 minutes. Serve with fried rice.

Prep time: 10 - 15 minutes
Cook time: 10 minutes

CRUNCHY TURKEY ESCALOPES

Replace the turkey breasts with chicken breasts or pieces of pork fillet for an equally tasty dish. Vary the flavour by using different stuffing mixes.

serves 4

ingredients	Metric	Imperial	American
Turkey breasts, boned	4	4	4
Egg, beaten	1	1	1
Packet parsley and thyme stuffing mix	90 g	3½ oz	1 cup
Oil for frying			
To garnish:			
Lemon wedges			
Watercress			
To serve:			
Puréed potatoes			
Green beans			

method

1. Put a turkey breast in a plastic bag. Beat with a rolling pin to flatten. Repeat with remaining pieces.

2. Dip turkey breasts in beaten egg, then stuffing mix to coat completely.

3. Shallow fry (sauté) in hot oil for about 3 minutes on each side until golden brown and cooked through.

4. Drain on kitchen paper. Transfer to warm serving plates. Garnish with lemon wedges and watercress and serve with puréed potatoes and green beans.

Prep time: 10 minutes
Cook time: 6 minutes

DUCK BREASTS À L'ORANGE

Two large duck breasts will be sufficient for four people - so this dish is not as extravagant as it may at first seem.

serves 4

ingredients

	Metric	Imperial	American
Large duck breasts	2	2	2
Salt and pepper			
Butter	25 g	1 oz	2 tbsp
Brandy	15 ml	1 tbsp	1 tbsp
Chicken stock	150 ml	¼ pt	⅔ cup
Soft brown sugar	5 ml	1 tsp	1 tsp
Orange, grated rind and juice	1	1	1
Cornflour (cornstarch)	15 ml	1 tbsp	1 tbsp
To garnish:			
Watercress			
Orange twists			
To serve:			
New potatoes			
Mangetout (snow peas)			

method

1. Remove skin from duck. Season the fillets, then fry (sauté) in butter turning occasionally for 15 minutes until just pink in the centre (or a little longer if you prefer it cooked well). Transfer to a warm dish and keep warm.

2. Add brandy to pan, ignite. When flames subside add stock and sugar. Blend orange rind and juice with cornflour. Stir into pan, bring to the boil stirring until thickened and clear. Season to taste.

3. Cut duck into neat slices. Arrange attractively on four warm serving plates. Spoon sauce over and garnish with watercress and orange twists. Serve with new potatoes and mangetout.

Prep time: 5 minutes
Cook time: about 18 minutes

FRAGRANT CHICKEN LIVERS

serves 4

ingredients	Metric	Imperial	American
Onions, chopped	2	2	2
Butter	25 g	1 oz	2 tbsp
Oil	10 ml	2 tsp	2 tsp
Wineglass medium sherry	1	1	1
Chicken livers, trimmed	450 g	1 lb	1 lb
Chopped sage	5 ml	1 tsp	1 tsp
Salt and pepper			
To serve:			
Buttered rice			
Leaf spinach			

method

1. Fry (sauté) onion in the butter and oil until soft and golden, about 3 minutes.

2. Add sherry and simmer, stirring until liquid has almost evaporated.

3. Add livers, sage and a little salt and pepper. Cook, stirring over a moderate heat until livers are cooked but still tender - about 5 minutes.

4. Serve with buttered rice and leaf spinach.

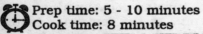
Prep time: 5 - 10 minutes
Cook time: 8 minutes

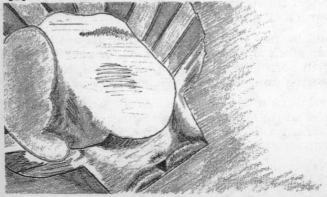

Spaghetti with Turkey and Mushrooms

serves 4

ingredients

	Metric	Imperial	American
Olive oil	60 ml	4 tbsp	4 tbsp
Boneless turkey, diced	175 g	6 oz	good 1 cup
Carrot, finely chopped	1	1	1
Celery stick (rib) finely chopped	1	1	1
Onion, finely chopped	1	1	1
Garlic clove, crushed	1	1	1
Button mushrooms, sliced	100 g	4 oz	2 cups
Tomatoes, chopped	4	4	4
Frozen peas	50 g	2 oz	½ cup
Spaghetti	350 g	12 oz	¾ lb
Salt and pepper			
To garnish:			
Parmesan cheese, grated			

method

1. Heat oil in a large pan. Fry (sauté) all ingredients except spaghetti for 3 minutes, stirring. Reduce heat, cover and cook gently for about 10 minutes stirring occasionally until cooked through.

2. Meanwhile cook spaghetti according to packet directions. Drain. Add to turkey mixture and toss well.

3. Serve hot with grated Parmesan cheese.

Prep time: 10 minutes
Cook time 13 - 15 minutes

SPANISH RICE

You can use up cooked chicken or turkey in this dish but the flavour won't be quite as good. Any leftovers taste delicious cold.

serves 4

ingredients	Metric	Imperial	American
Boneless chicken, diced	175 g	6 oz	good 1 cup
Small green (bell) pepper, diced	1	1	1
Small red (bell) pepper, diced	1	1	1
Olive oil	30 ml	2 tbsp	2 tbsp
Long-grain rice	225 g	8 oz	1 cup
Chicken stock	600 ml	1 pt	2½ cups
Frozen peas with sweetcorn (corn)	100 g	4 oz	1 cup
Peeled prawns (shrimp)	100 g	4 oz	⅔ cup
Salt and pepper			
To garnish:			
Black olives			
Chopped parsley			

method

1. Fry (sauté) chicken and peppers in the oil for 4 minutes, stirring.

2. Add rice and stir for one minute.

3. Pour on stock, bring to the boil, cover and simmer for 10 minutes.

4. Add peas and sweetcorn and prawns, re-cover and cook for a further 10 minutes until rice is cooked and has absorbed nearly all the liquid. Season to taste.

5. Serve garnished with olives and chopped parsley.

Prep time: 10 minutes
Cook time: 25 minutes

Meatless Meals

You don't have to be a vegetarian to enjoy meals without meat. The following recipes are all very nutritious and exceptionally tasty too.

Don't forget, if you are serving them to vegetarians, make sure you use vegetarian cheese or one that's suitable for them to eat (it's usually marked on the packet).

CAESAR SALAD SPECIAL

serves 4

ingredients

	Metric	Imperial	American
Butter	15 g	½ oz	1 tbsp
Egg, beaten	1	1	1
Soft garlic and herb cheese	75 g	3 oz	⅓ cup
Milk	45 ml	3 tbsp	3 tbsp
Olive oil	15 ml	1 tbsp	1 tbsp
Lemon juice	10 ml	2 tsp	2 tsp
Cos (romaine) lettuce	1	1	1
Small can anchovies, drained and chopped	1	1	1
French bread slices, fried (sautéed) in a little olive oil	8	8	8
To garnish:			
Tomato wedges			

method

1. Melt butter in a pan. Add egg and scramble lightly over a gentle heat. Remove from heat and leave to cool.

2. Whisk cheese with milk, oil and lemon juice until smooth.

3. Tear lettuce into neat pieces. Place in a salad bowl.

4. Add egg and anchovies, pour over dressing and toss.

5. Arrange slices of fried French bread around edges of bowl and garnish with tomato wedges.

Prep time: 15 minutes

Cucumber and Potato Gourmet

serves 4

ingredients

	Metric	Imperial	American
Potatoes, diced	450 g	1 lb	2⅔ cup
Cucumbers, cut in bite-sized chunks	2	2	2
White wine	150 ml	¼ pt	⅔ cup
Milk	300 ml	½ pt	1¼ cups
Butter or margarine	25 g	1 oz	2 tbsp
Plain (all-purpose) flour	25 g	1 oz	¼ cup
Cheddar cheese, grated	175 g	6 oz	1½ cups
Salt and pepper			
Dijon mustard	5 ml	1 tsp	1 tsp
To serve:			
Beetroot (red beets), walnut and celery salad			

method

1. Cook potatoes in boiling water until just tender about 4-5 minutes. Drain.
2. Put cucumber in a pan with the wine. Cover and cook for about 8-10 minutes until tender. Remove cucumber from wine with a draining spoon.
3. Add milk to wine then whisk in butter and flour. Bring to the boil and cook for 2 minutes, whisking all the time.
4. Stir in half the cheese and season to taste with salt, pepper and mustard. Fold in cooked potatoes and cucumber and heat through.
5. Turn into a lightly buttered flameproof dish and sprinkle with remaining cheese. Grill (broil) until golden and bubbling. Serve hot with beetroot, walnut and celery salad.

Prep time: 10 minutes
Cook time: 15 - 20 minutes

NO-NONSENSE RATATOUILLE

serves 4

ingredients	Metric	Imperial	American
Small aubergine (eggplant), sliced	1	1	1
Courgettes (zucchini) sliced	3	3	3
Onion, sliced	1	1	1
Green (bell) pepper, sliced	1	1	1
Tomatoes, chopped	4	4	4
Olive oil	45 ml	3 tbsp	3 tbsp
Dried oregano	2.5 ml	½ tsp	½ tsp
Salt and pepper			
Tomato purée (paste)	15 ml	1 tbsp	1 tbsp
Red wine or water	30 ml	2 tbsp	2 tbsp
To serve:			
Buttered pasta			
Parmesan cheese, grated			

method

1. Put prepared vegetables in a large pan with the olive oil. Cook, stirring for 5 minutes until they begin to soften.

2. Add herbs, seasoning, and tomato purée blended with the wine or water. Cover and simmer for 15 minutes, stirring occasionally until vegetables are just tender.

3. Serve with buttered pasta and grated Parmesan cheese.

Prep time: 10 minutes
Cook time: 20 minutes

PISSALADIÈRE

Use a processor to make the pastry in an instant

serves 4

ingredients	Metric	Imperial	American
Pastry (paste):			
Plain (all-purpose) flour	175 g	6 oz	1½ cups
Ground cinnamon	5 ml	1 tsp	1 tsp
Butter	75 g	3 oz	⅓ cup
Cold water to mix			
Filling:			
Onions, chopped	3	3	3
Garlic clove, crushed	1	1	1
Olive oil	30 ml	2 tbsp	2 tbsp
Tomatoes, roughly chopped	450 g	1 lb	1 lb
Tomato purée (paste)	15 ml	1 tbsp	1 tbsp
Caster (superfine) sugar	2.5 ml	½ tsp	½ tsp
Salt and pepper			
Small can anchovy fillets, drained	1	1	1
Black olives	6	6	6
To garnish:			
Chopped parsley			
To serve:			
Green salad			

method

1. Mix flour and cinnamon together. Rub in the butter and mix with enough cold water to form a firm dough.

2. Roll out and use to line a 20 cm/8 in flan dish (pie pan).

3. Prick base with a fork, add some crumpled foil and bake 'blind' for 8 minutes in a hot oven 200°C/400°F/gas mark 6. Remove foil and cook for a further 4 minutes.

4. Meanwhile, soften onion and garlic in the oil for 2

minutes in a large pan. Add tomatoes, stir, cover and cook for 8 minutes until pulpy. Stir in the tomato purée, sugar and a little salt and pepper.

5. Turn into pastry case. Spread out and decorate in a criss-cross pattern with the anchovies and the olives. Return to the oven for 10 minutes. Garnish with chopped parsley and serve with a green salad.

Prep time: 10 - 15 minutes
Cook time 22 minutes

PIZZA PARCELS

serves 4

ingredients

	Metric	Imperial	American
Filo pastry (paste) sheets	4	4	4
Butter, melted	15 g	½ oz	1 tbsp
Canned pimiento, chopped	1 piece	1 piece	1 piece
Mushrooms, sliced	4	4	4
Tomatoes, sliced	2	2	2
Basil leaves	8	8	8
Pepper			
Mozzarella cheese, grated	100 g	4 oz	1 cup
To garnish:			
Basil leaves			
Black olives			
To serve:			
Ciabatta bread			
Green salad			

method

1. Brush filo pastry with a very little butter. Fold in half and brush again.

2. Divide pimiento, mushrooms and tomato between the 4 pieces of pastry. Top with torn basil leaves, some pepper and the grated cheese.

3. Draw pastry up over filling to form parcels, squeezing between finger and thumb to secure. Transfer to a buttered baking sheet. Brush with remaining butter.

4. Bake in a hot oven 200°C/400°F/gas mark 6 for about 12 - 15 minutes until golden.

5. Transfer to warm plates. Garnish with basil leaves and olives and serve straight away with ciabatta bread and a green salad.

Prep time: 10 minutes
Cook time: 12 - 15 minutes

REGATTA RICE RING

serves 4

ingredients

	Metric	Imperial	American
Long-grain rice	175 g	6 oz	¾ cup
Frozen diced mixed vegetables	100 g	4 oz	1 cup
Olive oil	30 ml	2 tbsp	2 tbsp
Wine vinegar	15 ml	1 tbsp	1 tbsp
Salt and pepper			
Filling:			
Ripe pears, diced	2	2	2
Cheddar cheese, diced	175 g	6 oz	1½ cups
Head Florence fennel, chopped	1	1	1
Natural (plain) yoghurt	45 ml	3 tbsp	3 tbsp
To serve:			
Garlic bread (p. 173)			

method

1. Cook rice and mixed vegetables in plenty of boiling, lightly salted water for 10 minutes. Drain, rinse thoroughly with cold water and drain again.

2. Add oil, vinegar and a little salt and pepper to the rice and vegetables and toss well.

3. Spoon mixture into a 1.5 litres/2¼ pts/6 cups oiled ring mould (mold). Press down well and chill in freezer compartment while making filling.

4. Mix pears with the cheese and fennel (saving the green feathery leaves for decoration). Gently fold in yoghurt and season lightly.

5. Place a serving plate over the ring mould. Invert, give a good shake and remove mould. Pile cheese and pear mixture in centre and garnish with the fennel leaves before serving with garlic bread.

Prep time: 15 minutes
Cook time: 10 minutes

SICILIAN SALAD

This is delicious with the addition of prawns (shrimps) or tuna fish.

serves 4

ingredients	Metric	Imperial	American
Dwarf green beans, cooked whole	225 g	8 oz	½ lb
Baby new potatoes, cooked	225 g	8 oz	½ lb
Tomatoes, quartered	4	4	4
Eggs, hard boiled (hard cooked), quartered	3	3	3
Small onion, sliced in rings	1	1	1
Black or green olives	6	6	6
Olive oil	45 ml	3 tbsp	3 tbsp
Wine vinegar	15 ml	1 tbsp	1 tbsp
Salt and pepper			
Crisp lettuce			
Goat's cheese, dried	75 g	3 oz	¾ cup
To serve:			
Crusty bread			

method

1. Cut beans and potatoes in two or three pieces. Place in a bowl with remaining ingredients, except lettuce and cheese, and toss lightly.

2. Pile onto a bed of crisp lettuce and scatter cheese over. Serve with crusty bread.

Prep time: 10 minutes, plus cooking vegetables if necessary.

SPAGHETTI WITH GREEN HERBS AND MUSHROOMS

Replace the parsley, sage and oregano with fresh basil for another delicious and fragrant dish.

serves 4

ingredients

	Metric	Imperial	American
Butter	50 g	2 oz	¼ cup
Mushrooms, sliced	100 g	4 oz	2 cups
Garlic clove, crushed	1	1	1
Ground almonds	50 g	2 oz	½ cup
Parmesan cheese, grated	30 ml	2 tbsp	2 tbsp
Olive oil	30 ml	2 tbsp	2 tbsp
Chopped parsley	30 ml	2 tbsp	2 tbsp
Chopped sage	10 ml	2 tsp	2 tsp
Chopped oregano	15 ml	1 tbsp	1 tbsp
Salt and pepper			
Spaghetti	350 g	12 oz	¾ lb
To serve:			
Tomato and onion salad			

method

1. Melt half the butter in a pan and fry (sauté) mushrooms gently for 3 minutes. Put to one side.

2. Mash remaining butter with the garlic, almonds and cheese. Gradually work in the oil, herbs and seasoning.

3. Cook spaghetti according to packet directions. Drain, return to saucepan and add mushrooms and herb mixture.

4. Stir over a gentle heat until spaghetti is well coated in the sauce. Serve hot with a tomato and onion salad.

Prep time: 10 minutes
Cook time: 12 - 15 minutes

Watercress Roulade

This recipe also makes a delicious starter for six to eight people.

serves 4

ingredients	Metric	Imperial	American
Filling:			
Onion, chopped	1	1	1
Olive oil	15 ml	1 tbsp	1 tbsp
Tomatoes, chopped	4	4	4
Tomato purée (paste)	15 ml	1 tbsp	1 tbsp
Caster (superfine) sugar	5 ml	1 tsp	1 tsp
Roulade:			
Bunch watercress, chopped	1	1	1
Chopped (snipped) chives	15 ml	1 tbsp	1 tbsp
Parmesan cheese, grated	45 ml	3 tbsp	3 tbsp
Eggs, separated	4	4	4
To serve:			
Raisin, nut and rice salad			

method

1. Fry (sauté) onion in the oil for 2 minutes to soften. Add tomatoes, cover and cook gently for 5 minutes or until pulpy. Add purée and sugar and season to taste. Keep warm.

2. Meanwhile make roulade: Grease an 18 cm x 28 cm/7 in x 11 in Swiss (jelly) roll tin. Line with baking parchment.

3. Wash watercress and finely chop. Mix watercress with chives, 30ml/2 tbsp of the Parmesan and a little seasoning. Beat in egg yolks.

4. Whisk egg whites until stiff and fold into watercress mixture with a metal spoon.

5. Turn mixture into prepared tin, smooth surface and cook towards the top of a hot oven, 200°C/400°F/gas mark 6 for about 10 minutes until golden and firm to the touch.

6. Dust a sheet of baking parchment with remaining Parmesan. Turn roulade out onto this and remove lining paper, easing it away with a palatte knife. Spread with tomato mixture and roll up starting with a short end.

7. Transfer roulade to a warm serving dish and serve sliced with a raisin, nut and rice salad.

Prep time: 20 minutes
Cook time: 10 minutes

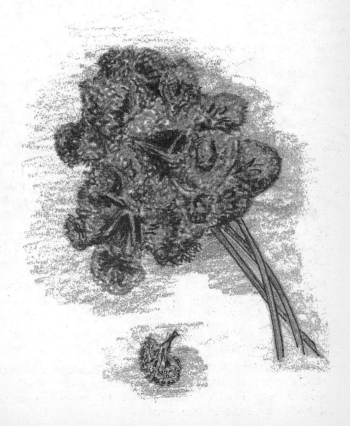

Snacks & Light Meals

When you fancy a quick bite you do not have to turn to pot noodles or cup-a-soups. Here is a range of tempting light lunch and supper dishes to show you that fast food can be fantastic.

CROQUE MADAME

serves 1

ingredients	Metric	Imperial	American
Slices bread	2	2	2
Butter			
Cheddar cheese, grated	40 g	1½ oz	3 tbsp
Small onion, sliced	½	½	½
Chopped sage	5 ml	1 tsp	1 tsp

method

1. Liberally butter slices of bread on one side.
2. Sandwich together, buttered sides out, with the cheese, onion (separated into rings), and sage.
3. Fry (sauté) or grill (broil) until golden on both sides. Serve straight away, cut into quarters.

Prep time: 3 - 5 minutes
Cook time 5 minutes

DEVILLED MUSHROOMS

serves 2

ingredients

	Metric	Imperial	American
Small onion, finely chopped	1	1	1
Oil	15 ml	1 tbsp	1 tbsp
Button mushrooms	175 g	6 oz	1½ cups
Tomatoes, skinned if liked, and chopped	2	2	2
Tomato ketchup (catsup)	10 ml	2 tsp	2 tsp
Worcestershire sauce	10 ml	2 tsp	2 tsp
Drops of Tabasco	1 - 2	1 - 2	1 - 2
To serve:			
Hot buttered toast			

method

1. Cook onion in the oil for 2 minutes until softened. Add mushrooms and tomatoes and cook, stirring for 2 minutes.
2. Add remaining ingredients and simmer for about 5 minutes or until mushrooms are just cooked.
3. Serve on hot buttered toast.

Prep time: 5 minutes
Cook time: 9 minutes

Macaroni Masterpiece

serves 2

ingredients	Metric	Imperial	American
Streaky bacon rashers (slices)	4	4	4
Quick-cook macaroni	100 g	4 oz	1 cup
Red Leicester cheese, grated	100 g	4 oz	1 cup
Worcestershire sauce	5 ml	1 tsp	1 tsp
Salt and pepper			
Butter, melted	25 g	1 oz	2 tbsp
To garnish:			
Chopped (snipped) chives			

method

1. Grill (broil) or dry-fry (sauté) bacon until crisp, cut into pieces.
2. Meanwhile cook macaroni according to packet directions, drain and return to pan.
3. Add cheese, Worcestershire sauce, a little seasoning and the butter. Toss well until creamy.
4. Pile onto warm serving plates and serve sprinkled with the bacon and chives.

Prep time: 5 minutes
Cook time: about 10 minutes

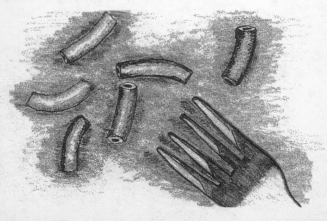

Melting Crescents

As an alternative you can spread the croissant with soft garlic and herb cheese and add some chopped red (bell) pepper before grilling (broiling).

serves 1

ingredients	Metric	Imperial	American
Croissant	1	1	1
Salami slices	2	2	2
Emmental or Gruyère cheese slice	1	1	1
To serve:			
Tomato slices			

method

1. Split croissant almost in half and fill with the folded salami and cheese slices.
2. Place under a moderate grill (broiler) until cheese melts, turning once.

Prep time: 2 minutes
Cook time: about 3 minutes

Pan Pizza

You can add additional toppings of your choice to this pizza like diced ham, sliced mushrooms, tuna etc.

serves 1 or 2 (depending on appetite)

ingredients	Metric	Imperial	American
Self-raising (self-rising) flour	100 g	4 oz	1 cup
Salt			
Sunflower oil	45 ml	3 tbsp	3 tbsp
Cold water			
Can chopped tomatoes, drained	227 g	8 oz	8 oz
Cheddar cheese, grated	50 g	2 oz	½ cup
Dried oregano	1.5 ml	¼ tsp	¼ tsp
To garnish:			
Black olives			

method

1. Mix flour, salt and 30 ml/2 tbsp of the oil in a bowl. Add enough water to form a firm dough and knead gently.

2. Roll or press out to a round to roughly fit base of a medium frying pan (skillet).

3. Heat remaining oil in frying pan, add dough and fry for one minute. Turn over and spread with tomatoes.

4. Top with cheese and sprinkle with oregano. Garnish with olives. Cover with a lid or foil and cook over a gentle heat for 5 minutes until cheese is melting. Place under a hot grill (broiler) to brown top.

Prep time: 8 - 10 minutes
Cook time: about 8 minutes

PIPIERADE

serves 2 - 4

ingredients	Metric	Imperial	American
Olive oil	15ml	1 tbsp	1 tbsp
Butter	15g	½ oz	1 tbsp
Onions, sliced	2	2	2
Green (bell) peppers, sliced	2	2	2
Large tomatoes, quartered	4	4	4
Garlic clove, crushed	1	1	1
Eggs, beaten	4	4	4
Salt and pepper			

method

1. Heat oil and butter in a large frying pan (skillet).
2. Add prepared vegetables and garlic and fry (sauté) gently for 5 minutes, stirring until soft.
3. Add eggs, season and cook, lifting and stirring gently until set. Serve straight from the pan.

Prep time: 5 - 10 minutes
Cook time: 10 minutes

Pitta Pocket Cooler

serves 1

ingredients	Metric	Imperial	American
Piece cucumber, chopped	2.5 cm	1 in	1 in
Cooked lamb, chopped	15 ml	1 tbsp	1 tbsp
Natural (plain) yoghurt	15 ml	1 tbsp	1 tbsp
Mint, dried	1.5 ml	¼ tsp	¼ tsp
Salt and pepper			
Pitta bread	1	1	1
Lettuce			
Tomato, sliced	1	1	1

method

1. Mix cucumber, lamb, yoghurt and mint together. Season to taste.
2. Warm pitta bread briefly under the grill (broiler) or in a toaster if liked.
3. Make a slit along one edge to form a pocket. Fill with lettuce leaves then add the yoghurt mixture and some tomato slices.

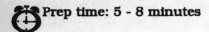Prep time: 5 - 8 minutes

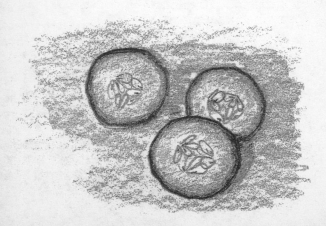

Saucy Ham 'n Eggs

serves 2

ingredients

	Metric	Imperial	American
Bunch watercress, chopped	1	1	1
Butter or margarine	15 g	½ oz	1 tbsp
Plain (all-purpose) flour	15 g	½ oz	1 tbsp
Milk	150 ml	¼ pt	⅔ cup
Salt and pepper			
Eggs	2	2	2
Lemon juice or vinegar	5 ml	1 tsp	1 tsp
Ham slices	2	2	2
Buttered toast slices	2	2	2

method

1. Put watercress, fat, flour and milk in a saucepan. Whisk over a moderate heat until thickened and smooth. Season to taste.
2. Poach eggs in water with the lemon juice or vinegar added, for 3 - 5 minutes to the consistency you like.
3. Put a slice of ham on each of the slices of toast.
4. Top with poached egg. Spoon hot watercress sauce over and serve straight away.

Prep time: 5 - 10 minutes
Cook time: 5 minutes

SOMERSET RAREBIT

You can substitute beer or white wine for the cider. Double the quantity for a quick cheese fondue to serve with cubes of French bread.

serves 1 or 2

ingredients	Metric	Imperial	American
Cheddar cheese, grated	175 g	6 oz	1½ cups
English mustard, made	5 ml	1 tsp	1 tsp
Cider	30 ml	2 tbsp	2 tbsp
Toast slices	2	2	2

method

1. Put all ingredients except toast in a small pan. Heat gently, stirring until cheese has melted and mixture is well blended.
2. Spoon onto toast and serve.

Prep time: 5 minutes
Cook time: about 5 minutes

SPICY POTATO CAKES

These potato cakes also make a delicious starter for four people, served before Tandoori Fish, Eastern Lamb or Chicken and Coconut Masala.

serves 2

ingredients	Metric	Imperial	American
Potatoes, grated	225 g	8 oz	2 cups
Small onion, grated	1	1	1
Garam masala	2.5 ml	½ tsp	½ tsp
Chilli (chili) powder	1.5 ml	¼ tsp	¼ tsp
Egg, beaten	1	1	1
Plain (all-purpose) flour	5 ml	1 tsp	1 tsp
Salt and pepper			
Oil	30 ml	2 tbsp	2 tbsp
To serve:			
Mango chutney			

method

1. Mix potato, onion, spices, egg and flour together.
2. Heat oil in a frying pan (skillet) and fry (sauté) tablespoons of the mixture until golden brown underneath. Turn over and fry other side for 4 - 5 minutes in all.
3. Serve hot with mango chutney.

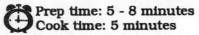
Prep time: 5 - 8 minutes
Cook time: 5 minutes

TORTILLA

This can be made with left over cooked potato. Tortilla is delicious served cold with salad.

serves 2

ingredients	Metric	Imperial	American
Large potato, cut in small dice	1	1	1
Small onion, chopped	1	1	1
Olive oil	15 ml	1 tbsp	1 tbsp
Chopped parsley	15 ml	1 tbsp	1 tbsp
Salt and pepper			
Eggs, beaten	4	4	4

method

1. Put potato and onion with the oil in a frying pan (skillet) and fry (sauté) for 4 minutes, stirring until potato is almost cooked.
2. Add parsley, a little seasoning and the eggs. Cook gently lifting and stirring at first until egg has almost set. Place under a hot grill (broiler) to brown and set top. Serve cut in wedges.

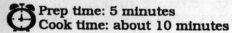
Prep time: 5 minutes
Cook time: about 10 minutes

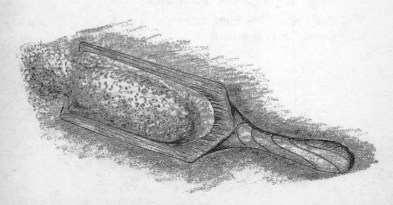

Desserts

For many people the crowning glory of the meal is the dessert. It may be hot or cold, rich or fruity but most of all it should be easy to make and look and taste superb.

BANANAS WITH HOT LEMON BUTTER SAUCE

Use ice-cream instead of yoghurt if you prefer.

serves 4

ingredients	Metric	Imperial	American
Butter	50 g	2 oz	¼ cup
Soft brown sugar	75 g	3 oz	⅓ cup
Lemon juice	30 ml	2 tbsp	2 tbsp
Greek-style natural (plain) yoghurt	300 ml	½ pt	1¼ cups
Bananas	4	4	4
To decorate:			
Toasted flaked almonds			

method

1. Put butter, sugar and lemon juice in a small pan. Heat gently, stirring until sugar has melted. Simmer for one minute.

2. Divide yoghurt between 4 sundae glasses. Top with sliced bananas.

3. Spoon sauce over and decorate with toasted almonds. Serve straight away.

Prep time: 5 minutes
Cook time: about 3 minutes

CARIBBEAN BANANAS

serves 4

ingredients

	Metric	Imperial	American
Orange	1	1	1
Cocoa (unsweetened chocolate) powder	45 ml	3 tbsp	3 tbsp
Soft brown sugar	45 ml	3 tbsp	3 tbsp
Ground cinnamon	pinch	pinch	pinch
Rum or orange liqueur	45 ml	3 tbsp	3 tbsp
Bananas	4	4	4
To serve:			
Whipped cream or fromage frais			

method

1. Cut 4 slices from orange for decoration. Grate rind and squeeze juice from remainder into a frying pan (skillet).

2. Add cocoa powder and sugar and heat gently until sugar melts. Add rum or orange liqueur.

3. Peel bananas and cut into chunky pieces. Add to pan. Spoon over sauce, cover with foil or a lid and cook gently for 4 minutes or until bananas are just cooked but still hold their shape.

4. Spoon into serving dishes, decorate with slices of orange and serve hot or cold with whipped cream or fromage frais.

Prep time: 5 minutes
Cook time: about 8 minutes

BLACKBERRY AND APPLE LAYER

When blackberries are not in season, use canned or frozen fruit instead.

serves 4 - 6

ingredients	Metric	Imperial	American
Cooking (tart) apples, sliced	450 g	1 lb	1 lb
Blackberries	100 g	4 oz	scant 1 cup
Sugar			
Trifle sponge cakes	4	4	4
Cider or apple juice	30 ml	2 tbsp	2 tbsp
Whipping cream	150 ml	1/4 pt	2/3 cup
Vanilla-flavoured thick yoghurt	300 ml	1/2 pt	1 1/4 cups

method

1. Put apples in a pan. Choose a few blackberries for decoration, if liked, then add remainder to pan with 15 ml/1 tbsp water. Cover and cook gently until just soft and the juice has run - about 5 minutes. Sweeten to taste.

2. Crumble trifle sponges into a glass serving bowl. Add fruit, drizzle cider or apple juice over. Leave to cool.

3. Whip cream and fold in yoghurt. Spread over fruit and decorate with reserved blackberries if liked.

Prep time: 10 minutes, plus cooling time
Cook time: 5 minutes

Caramel Apples

serves 4

ingredients

	Metric	Imperial	American
Butter	50 g	2 oz	¼ cup
Eating (dessert) apples, sliced	4	4	4
Soft light brown sugar	50 g	2 oz	¼ cup
Mixed (apple pie) spice	2.5 ml	½ tsp	½ tsp
Sultanas (golden raisins)	25 g	1 oz	2 tbsp
Walnuts or pecans, chopped	25 g	1 oz	¼ cup
To serve:			
Whipped cream or Greek-style yoghurt			

method

1. Melt butter in a frying pan (skillet).
2. Add apples and sprinkle with sugar. Fry (sauté) tossing occasionally for about 3 minutes until sugar has melted.
3. Add sultanas and nuts and toss gently. Serve with whipped cream or Greek-style yoghurt.

⏰ Prep time: 5 minutes
Cook time: 5 minutes

Chocolate-Dipped Delights

serves 4

ingredients

	Metric	Imperial	American
Plain (semi-sweet) chocolate	175 g	6 oz	1 cup
Ripe nectarines or peaches, sliced	4	4	4
Sweetened whipped cream or crème fraîche	150 ml	1/4 pt	2/3 cup
A little grated chocolate (optional)			

method

1. Melt chocolate in a bowl over a pan of hot water or in the microwave.
2. Dip fruit in the chocolate to come halfway up each slice.
3. Arrange on serving plates in a starburst pattern and put a spoonful of sweetened whipped cream or crème fraîche in the middle. Top this with a little grated chocolate, if liked.

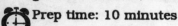 Prep time: 10 minutes

Chocolate Mousse

To make chocolate curls, scrape a potato peeler along the edge of a bar of chocolate several times.

serves 6

ingredients	Metric	Imperial	American
Plain (semi-sweet) chocolate	200 g	7 oz	good 1 cup
Eggs, separated	3	3	3
Brandy	15 ml	1 tbsp	1 tbsp
Whipping cream	150 ml	¼ pt	⅔ cup
To decorate:			
Chocolate curls			

method

1. Melt chocolate over a pan of hot water or in the microwave. Beat in the egg yolks and brandy.

2. Whisk egg whites and then the cream until peaking (this means you do not have to wash beaters in between). Fold cream, then egg whites into the mixture.

3. Turn into a serving dish, sprinkle with chocolate curls and chill until ready to serve.

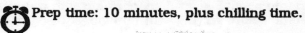Prep time: 10 minutes, plus chilling time.

Coffee Cream Cheese Italienne

This dessert needs to be very cold. If you have not time to chill it in the fridge for a couple of hours, pop it in the freezer for 15 minutes or so before serving.

serves 6

ingredients	Metric	Imperial	American
Instant coffee granules	15 g	½ oz	1 tbsp
Water	15 ml	1 tbsp	1 tbsp
Cream cheese	225 g	8 oz	1 cup
Icing (confectioners') sugar, sifted	100 g	4 oz	½ cup
To decorate:			
Chopped walnuts			
To serve:			
Thin ginger biscuits (cookies)			

method

1. Blend coffee and water together until dissolved.
2. Gradually beat into cream cheese with the icing sugar.
3. Turn into a small glass dish, sprinkle with walnuts and chill before serving with thin ginger biscuits.

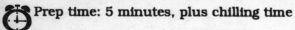
Prep time: 5 minutes, plus chilling time

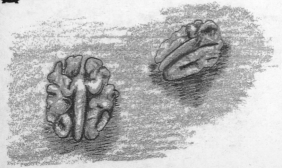

Fresh Fruit Platter with Raspberry Sauce

serves 6

ingredients

	Metric	Imperial	American
Raspberry Sauce:			
Raspberries (fresh or frozen, thawed)	225 g	8 oz	½ lb
Icing (confectioners') sugar	25 g	1 oz	2 tbsp
Lemon juice	15 ml	1 tbsp	1 tbsp
A selection of sliced fresh fruits, e.g. star fruit, mango, pawpaw, strawberries, kiwifruit			
To serve:			
Ratafias			

method

1. Purée raspberries with the sugar and lemon juice in a blender or processor then pass through a sieve to remove seeds.

2. Spoon a little of the sauce onto each of 6 serving plates. Arrange slices of fruit attractively around. Serve with ratafias.

Prep time: 15 minutes

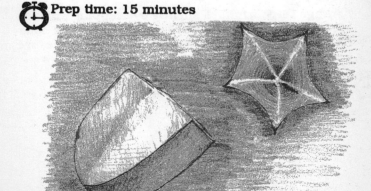

FRINKLIES

Pop these in the oven when you dish up the main course as they're best eaten freshly cooked.

serves 4

ingredients	Metric	Imperial	American
Soft margarine	50 g	2 oz	¼ cup
Caster (superfine) sugar	50 g	2 oz	¼ cup
Eggs	2	2	2
Plain (all-purpose) flour	50 g	2 oz	½ cup
Milk	150 ml	¼ pt	⅔ cup
Warm jam or clear honey			
Icing (confectioners') sugar			

method

1. Beat fat, sugar, eggs and flour together then stir in the milk. (Do not worry if the mixture curdles).

2. Spoon into 12 sections of a greased bun tin (muffin pan).

3. Bake in a hot oven, 200°C/400°F/gas mark 6 for about 15 - 20 minutes until set and golden. They will sink when they're taken out of the oven - but don't worry, they're supposed to!

4. Arrange three frinklies slightly overlapping on each serving plate. Spoon a little warmed jam or clear honey over and dust with icing sugar before serving.

Prep time: 5 minutes
Cooking time: 15 - 20 minutes

Fruit Brulée

You can also use sliced stone fruit like peaches, plums or nectarines.

serves 4

ingredients	Metric	Imperial	American
Strawberries, sliced or raspberries	225 g	8 oz	good 1½ cups
Double (heavy) cream	150 ml	¼ pt	⅔ cup
Thick natural (plain) yoghurt	150 ml	¼ pt	⅔ cup
Demerara (light brown) sugar			

method

1. Arrange fruit in a shallow flameproof dish.
2. Whip cream and yoghurt together until softly peaking. Spread over fruit.
3. Sprinkle liberally with demerara sugar, so it covers the top completely.
4. Place under a very hot grill (broiler) until sugar melts. Serve straight away.

Prep time: 5 minutes
Cook time: about 3 minutes

Greek Yoghurt Surprise

serves 4

ingredients	Metric	Imperial	American
Dried no-need-to-soak apricots, chopped	100 g	4 oz	⅔ cup
Brandy	30 ml	2 tbsp	2 tbsp
Greek-style yoghurt	450 ml	¾ pt	2 cups
Clear honey			

method

1. Mix apricots and brandy together and place in 4 glass dishes.
2. Spoon on yoghurt, then top with a layer of clear honey.

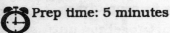Prep time: 5 minutes

JALOUSIE

serves 6 - 8

ingredients	Metric	Imperial	American
Puff pastry (paste) thawed if frozen Black cherry jam Milk to glaze **To decorate:** Icing (confectioners') sugar, sifted **To serve:** Whipped cream	225 g	8 oz	½ lb

method

1. Cut pastry in half and roll one half out to a rectangle about 20 cm x 25 cm/8 in x 10 in. Transfer to a dampened baking sheet.
2. Roll out other half to the same size. Dust with a little flour then fold in half, lengthwise. Make a series of cuts along folded edge to within 2.5 cm/1 in of open edge (like when you made paper lanterns as a child).
3. Spread uncut rectangle generously with jam, leaving a 2.5 cm/1 in border all round. Brush edge with water then carefully unfold the cut rectangle and lay over the top, pressing edges well together to seal.
4. Bake in a hot oven 220°C/425°F/gas mark 7 for about 15 minutes until golden and puffy. Dust with icing sugar and serve warm with whipped cream.

Prep time: 10 - 15 minutes
Cook time: 15 minutes

Lemon Dream

Eaten straight away, this dessert is creamy and light. Chill for several hours and you'll have a syllabub-effect: fluffy on the top, juicy underneath.

serves 6

ingredients	Metric	Imperial	American
Egg white	1	1	1
Caster (superfine) sugar	75 g	3 oz	⅓ cup
Double (heavy) cream	150 ml	¼ pt	⅔ cup
Lemon, grated rind and juice	1	1	1
Natural (plain) thick yoghurt	300 ml	½ pt	1¼ cups
To decorate:			
Crystallised (candied) violets or lemon slices			
Angelica 'leaves'			

method

1. Whisk egg white until stiff then whisk in half the sugar.

2. Whip cream, lemon rind and juice and remaining sugar until softly peaking. Gently whisk or fold in yoghurt. Finally fold in egg white with a metal spoon.

3. Spoon into 6 wine goblets and chill if liked. Just before serving, top each with a crystallised violet or lemon slice and an angelica leaf.

Prep time: 10 minutes, plus chilling if liked

MANGO FOOL

This dessert is best eaten soon after it is made.

serves 4
ingredients

	Metric	Imperial	American
Mango	1	1	1
Lemon juice	45 ml	3 tbsp	3 tbsp
Caster (superfine) sugar	15 ml	1 tbsp	1 tbsp
Can custard	425 g	15 oz	15 oz
Whipped cream	150 ml	¼ pt	⅔ cup
To decorate:			
Angelica 'leaves'			

method

1. Peel and cut all flesh off mango stone (pit). Purée in a blender or processor with the lemon juice and sugar.
2. Fold in custard and half the cream.
3. Spoon into 4 wine goblets. Decorate each with a swirl of remaining whipped cream and an angelica leaf. Eat within 2 hours.

 Prep time: 10 minutes

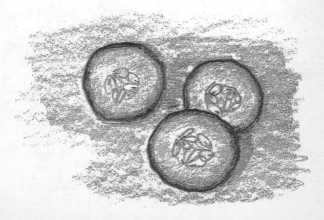

MELON GLACÉ

Ginger or raspberry ripple ice cream also go well with melon.

serves 4

ingredients	Metric	Imperial	American
Small ogen, cantaloupe, galia or charentais melons	2	2	2
Vanilla ice cream scoops	4	4	4
Ginger wine	30 ml	2 tbsp	2 tbsp

method

1. Cut melons in half, scoop out and discard the seeds (pits). Place in 4 individual serving dishes.

2. Add a scoop of ice cream to the cavity in the centre of each and spoon ginger wine over. Serve straight away.

Prep time: 5 minutes

Minted Melon and Raspberries

serves 6

ingredients

	Metric	Imperial	American
Honeydew melon	1	1	1
Raspberries	225 g	8 oz	good 1½ cups
Mint leaves	12	12	12
Granulated sugar	50 g	2 oz	¼ cup
To decorate:			
Mint sprig			

method

1. Cut melon in half, remove seeds (pits) then scoop out flesh with a melon baller. Alternatively, peel the melon and dice the flesh. Mix with the raspberries in a glass serving dish.

2. Put mint on a board with the sugar and chop finely. Sprinkle over fruit and chill until ready to serve, decorated with a sprig of mint.

Prep time: 10 minutes, Plus chilling time

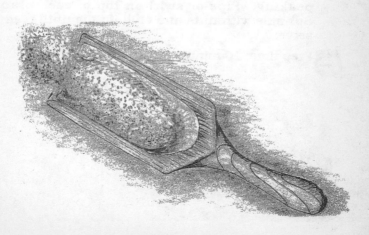

ORANGE RAFFLES

serves 6

ingredients	Metric	Imperial	American
Oranges	6	6	6
Trifle sponges	3	3	3
Sherry	30 ml	2 tbsp	2 tbsp
Double (heavy) or whipping cream	250 ml	8 fl oz	1 cup
Vanilla essence (extract)	few drops	few drops	few drops
Caster (superfine) sugar	30 ml	2 tbsp	2 tbsp
To decorate:			
Flaked almonds, toasted			

method

1. Cut rounded ends off oranges, (they will stand up better on the stalk end) and scoop out flesh with a serrated knife.

2. Chop fairly finely and place in a bowl with any juice.

3. Crumble in trifle sponges and add sherry. Mix well and spoon back into orange shells.

4. Whip cream with sugar and vanilla until softly peaking. Pipe or swirl on top of each orange. Sprinkle with nuts and chill if time until ready to serve.

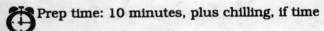Prep time: 10 minutes, plus chilling, if time

Pear and Ginger Strudels

If you don't like ginger, try substituting chocolate chips instead.

serves 4

ingredients	Metric	Imperial	American
Ripe pears, chopped	2	2	2
Pieces stem ginger in syrup, chopped	2	2	2
Filo pastry sheets	4	4	4
Melted butter	15 g	½ oz	1 tbsp

method

1. Mix pears and ginger together.
2. Brush sheets of pastry with a little butter, fold in half and brush with a little more butter.
3. Divide mixture between sheets of pastry, putting it in the middle of one edge. Fold pastry either side over filling then roll up. Brush with any remaining butter.
4. Transfer to a lightly buttered baking sheet and bake in a moderately hot oven, 190°C/375°F/gas mark 5 for 10 - 15 minutes until golden. Serve warm with a little syrup from the jar of ginger spooned over.

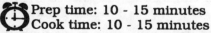
Prep time: 10 - 15 minutes
Cook time: 10 - 15 minutes

Pink Grapefruit Cheesecake

This recipe is equally delicious with other citrus fruit. If you have not time to chill the cheesecake in the fridge, pop it in the freezer compartment for 15 minutes instead.

serves 6

ingredients	Metric	Imperial	American
Chocolate digestive biscuits (graham crackers), crushed	200g	7 oz	scant 2 cups
Butter, melted	50 g	2 oz	¼ cup
Curd (smooth cottage) cheese	500 g	1 lb 2 oz	2¼ cups
Icing (confectioners') sugar, sifted	40 g	1½ oz	3 tbsp
Pink grapefruit, grated rind and juice	1	1	1
Lemon juice	15ml	1 tbsp	1 tbsp
Ground almonds	50 g	2 oz	½ cup
To decorate:			
Chocolate, grated			

method

1. Mix biscuits with the butter and press into a lightly buttered 18 - 20 cm/7 - 8 in flan dish.

2. Beat cheese, sugar, rind and juice of grapefruit, lemon juice and almonds together. Spoon over biscuit base.

3. Top with a little grated chocolate and chill until ready to serve (allow 30 minutes, preferably longer).

Prep time: 15 minutes, plus chilling time.

SPARKLING NECTARINES

Use peaches or other soft fruit instead of nectarines if you prefer.

serves 4

ingredients	Metric	Imperial	American
Nectarines	4	4	4
Bottle sparkling medium-sweet wine, chilled	½	½	½

method

1. Halve and slice nectarines, discarding stones (pits). Divide between 4 champagne cups or wine goblets. Chill.

2. Just before serving, top up with chilled sparkling wine. (Eat the fruit with a spoon then sip the wine).

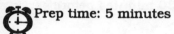Prep time: 5 minutes

Strawberry and Peach Romanoff

serves 6

ingredients	Metric	Imperial	American
Strawberries, sliced	225 g	8 oz	good 1½ cups
Peaches, stoned, (pitted) and sliced	4	4	4
Caster (superfine) sugar	15 ml	1 tbsp	1 tbsp
Peach or orange liqueur	30 ml	2 tbsp	2 tbsp
Orange juice, freshly squeezed	45 ml	3 tbsp	3 tbsp
To serve: Whipped cream			

method

1. Put prepared fruit in a glass bowl. Sprinkle with sugar and pour over the liqueur and orange juice.

2. Leave to stand for 20 - 30 minutes before serving with whipped cream.

Prep time: 10 minutes, plus standing time.

Strawberry Syllabub

If you have time to chill this dessert for several hours before serving, it will separate into two luscious layers.

serves 6

ingredients	Metric	Imperial	American
Strawberries, hulled	350 g	12 oz	scant 2½ cups
Caster (superfine) sugar	100 g	4 oz	½ cup
Lemon juice	15 ml	1 tbsp	1 tbsp
Dry white wine	150 ml	¼ pt	⅔ cup
Double (heavy) cream	300 ml	½ pt	1¼ cups

method

1. Purée fruit in a blender or processor.
2. Put remaining ingredients in a bowl and whisk until softly peaking.
3. Fold in strawberry purée gently with a metal spoon. Spoon into 6 wine goblets. Chill if possible before serving.

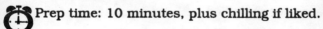
Prep time: 10 minutes, plus chilling if liked.

Toffee Plum Charlotte

serves 4

ingredients	Metric	Imperial	American
Butter	50 g	2 oz	¼ cup
Soft brown sugar	225 g	8 oz	1 cup
Lemon juice	15 ml	1 tbsp	1 tbsp
Slices of bread, cut thickly from a large loaf, crusts removed and cubed	4	4	4
Ripe plums, quartered and stones (pits) removed	450 g	1 lb	1 lb
To serve:			
Double (heavy) cream			

method

1. Melt butter in a large heavy-based frying pan (skillet). Add sugar and stir over a gently heat until sugar has dissolved. Add lemon juice.

2. Gently fold bread through toffee mixture until completely coated. Add plums, cover and cook for about 5 minutes until the fruit is soft.

3. Serve hot or chilled with thick cream.

Prep time: 10 - 15 minutes
Cook time: 8 - 10 minutes

TROPICANA DELIGHT

serves 4

ingredients	Metric	Imperial	American
Fresh pineapple	1	1	1
Fresh dates quartered and stoned (pitted)	75 g	3 oz	½ cup
Small bananas, sliced	2	2	2
Soft brown sugar	25 g	1 oz	2 tbsp
Apple juice	45 ml	3 tbsp	3 tbsp
Dark rum	45 ml	3 tbsp	3 tbsp

method

1. Cut top off pineapple about 3 cm/1¼ in from the leaves and reserve to use as a lid.
2. Scoop our pineapple flesh with a serrated knife, leaving skin intact. Chop flesh, discarding any hard core.
3. Put in a bowl with the dates and bananas. Toss lightly.
4. Blend sugar, apple juice and rum together until sugar has dissolved. Add to bowl and toss well. Spoon fruit and juice back into pineapple shell, replace lid and chill, if time, before serving.

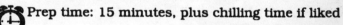 Prep time: 15 minutes, plus chilling time if liked

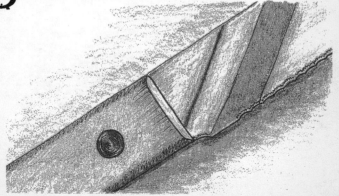

ZABAGLIONE

This dish was originally made with Marsala wine, but sweet sherry makes a very good alternative.

serves 4

ingredients	Metric	Imperial	American
Eggs	2	2	2
Caster (superfine) sugar	25 g	1 oz	2 tbsp
Sweet sherry	45 ml	3 tbsp	3 tbsp
To serve:			
Sponge fingers			

method

1. Put ingredients in a deep bowl over a pan of hot water. Whisk until thick and creamy - a hand-held electric mixer is easiest, but a balloon whisk will give larger volume.
2. Pour the Zabaglione into glasses and serve straight away with sponge fingers.

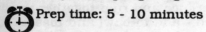 Prep time: 5 - 10 minutes

Quick Breads, Biscuits & Cakes

Here is a miscellany of bakes from appetising breads to serve with starters or main courses, through to tempting sweetmeats to serve with coffee. There are also some teatime treats to impress your family and friends.

CORNMEAL PANCAKES

Serve these with quick chilli (p.76), baked beans and grated cheese, crumbled bacon and scrambled egg, or any other savoury combination. Simply spoon on, roll up and eat with fingers.

makes 8 - 10

ingredients	Metric	Imperial	American
Plain (all-purpose) flour	100 g	4 oz	1 cup
Salt	1.5 ml	¼ tsp	¼ tsp
Cornmeal	50 g	2 oz	½ cup
Water	375 ml	13 fl oz	1½ cups
Egg, beaten	1	1	1
Oil for greasing			

method

1. Whisk all ingredients together in a bowl until smooth.
2. Heat a small, lightly oiled frying pan (skillet). Add about 45 ml/3 tbsp batter to coat base thickly. Fry (sauté) over a moderate heat, swirling pan gently until pancake is dry but edges are not brown. Turn over and cook other side briefly.
3. Keep warm on a plate over a pan of hot water while cooking remainder. Serve warm.

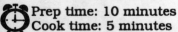
Prep time: 10 minutes
Cook time: 5 minutes

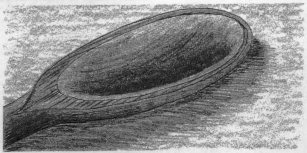

Garlic Bread

For a milder flavour, use only one garlic clove.

serves 6

ingredients	Metric	Imperial	American
Butter	100 g	4 oz	½ cup
Garlic cloves, crushed	2	2	2
Small French stick	1	1	1

method

1. Blend together the butter and garlic.
2. Cut French stick into 12 slices, not quite slicing through bottom crust, to keep loaf intact.
3. Spread butter mixture between slices and over top. Wrap in foil and bake in a hot oven, 200°C/400°F/gas mark 6 for about 15 minutes until crust feels crisp but centre is still soft.

variation

GARLIC ROLLS: Spread butter mixture in 6 white or wholemeal rolls or bagels. Wrap in foil, shiny side in. Bake as above or grill (broil) turning once for 15 minutes.

Prep time: 5 - 10 minutes
Cook time: 15 minutes

HERBY PITTAS

serves 6

ingredients

	Metric	Imperial	American
Pitta breads	3	3	3
Butter	65 g	2½ oz	5 tbsp
Mixed herbs (parsley, chives and marjoram are good), chopped	30 ml	2 tbsp	2 tbsp
OR			
Dried mixed herbs	15 ml	1 tbsp	1 tbsp
Garlic salt (optional)	5 ml	1 tsp	1 tsp

method

1. Cut pittas in half widthwise and split open along cut edge to form pockets.
2. Mash butter and herbs together with garlic salt, if using. Spread inside pockets.
3. Place under a hot grill (broiler) for 2 minutes on each side until bread is crisp and golden and butter has melted.

variation

HOT HERB LOAF: Make double the quantity of herb butter. Slice a small French stick into 12, not quite cutting through bottom crust. Spread butter mixture between slices and over top. Wrap in foil and bake in a hot oven, 200°C/400°F/gas mark 6 for about 15 minutes until crust feels crisp when squeezed.

Prep time: 5 minutes
Cook time: 4 minutes (pittas) 15 minutes (loaf)

Hot Walnut Bread

serves 6

ingredients	Metric	Imperial	American
Walnut halves	50 g	2 oz	½ cup
Chopped parsley	15 ml	1 tbsp	1 tbsp
Butter	50 g	2 oz	¼ cup
Garlic salt	5 ml	1 tsp	1 tsp
Small French stick	1	1	1

method

1. Grind nuts in a blender or processor. Add remaining ingredients, except the bread, and blend well.
2. Slice French stick into 12, not quite cutting through bottom crust. Spread nut mixture between slices and over top.
3. Wrap in foil and bake in a hot oven, 200°C/400°F/gas mark 6 for 15 minutes until crust feels crisp when squeezed.

Prep time: 5 minutes
Cook time: 15 minutes

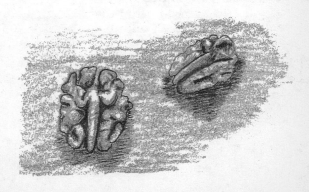

OATMEAL BANNOCKS

makes 6

ingredients

	Metric	Imperial	American
Wholemeal (graham) flour	175 g	6 oz	1½ cups
Baking powder	15 ml	1 tbsp	1 tbsp
Salt	2.5 ml	½ tsp	½ tsp
Fine oatmeal	50 g	2 oz	½ cup
Caster (superfine) sugar	15 ml	1 tbsp	1 tbsp
Margarine	25 g	1 oz	2 tbsp
Water	150 g	¼ pt	⅔ cup
To serve:			
Butter			

method

1. Mix dry ingredients together, then rub in the margarine.
2. Mix with enough water to form a soft, but not sticky dough. Knead gently and form into 6 flat cakes about 1 cm/½ in thick.
3. Cook on a griddle or in a hot non-stick frying pan (skillet) for about 5 minutes on each side until well risen and golden brown. Serve warm, split and buttered.

Prep time: 10 minutes
Cook time: 10 minutes

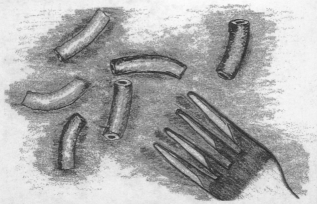

Quick Cheese Soda Bread

If you run out of bread and want to make a quick plain loaf, simply omit the cheese and mustard.

ingredients	Metric	Imperial	American
Plain (all-purpose) flour	450 g	1 lb	4 cups
Bicarbonate of soda (baking soda)	10 ml	2 tsp	2 tsp
Cream of tartar	10 ml	2 tsp	2 tsp
Salt	5ml	1 tsp	1 tsp
Mustard powder (optional)	2.5ml	½ tsp	½ tsp
Butter or margarine	25g	1 oz	2 tbsp
Strong Cheddar cheese, grated	100g	4 oz	1 cup
Milk	300ml	½ pt	1¼ cups
To serve:			
Butter			

method

1. Sift dry ingredients into a bowl. Rub in the butter.
2. Stir in the cheese and enough of the milk to form a soft, but not sticky dough.
3. Shape into a ball on a lightly floured surface.
4. Transfer to a baking sheet, flatten slightly and mark into quarters with a knife.
5. Bake in a hot oven, 220°C/425°F/gas mark 7 for 20 - 25 minutes until risen, golden and base sounds hollow when tapped. Cool slightly then break into quarters and thickly slice before serving with butter.

Prep time: 10 minutes
Cook time: 20 - 25 minutes

RYE SCOTCH PANCAKES

makes about 24

ingredients	Metric	Imperial	American
Rye flour	100 g	4 oz	1 cup
Salt	pinch	pinch	pinch
Caster (superfine) sugar	10 ml	2 tsp	2 tsp
Eggs, separated	2	2	2
Milk	300 ml	½ pt	1¼ cups
Oil for frying			
To serve:			
Butter and honey			

method

1. Mix flour, salt and sugar together.
2. Add egg yolks and gradually beat in the milk.
3. Whisk egg whites until peaking and fold into batter with a metal spoon.
4. Heat a little oil in a large frying pan (skillet). Pour off excess oil. Put tablespoons of the batter into the pan a few at a time and cook on each side until golden.
5. Keep warm in a clean cloth while cooking remainder. Serve warm with butter and honey.

Prep time: 10 minutes
Cook time: about 20 minutes

SAVOURY WHOLEMEAL ROLLS

These rolls are delicious served with cheese and pickles or as an accompaniment to any soup.

makes 10

ingredients	Metric	Imperial	American
Wholemeal (graham) flour	225 g	8 oz	2 cups
Plain (all-purpose) flour	50 g	2 oz	½ cup
Baking powder	20 ml	4 tsp	4 tsp
Salt	1.5 ml	¼ tsp	¼ tsp
Dried onions, crumbled	15 g	½ oz	1 tbsp
Mixed dried herbs	2.5 ml	½ tsp	½ tsp
Oil	30 ml	2 tbsp	2 tbsp
Natural (plain) yoghurt	150 ml	¼ pt	⅔ cup
Milk			

method

1. Mix all the dry ingredients together in a bowl. Stir in the oil.
2. Mix with yoghurt and just enough milk to form a soft, but not sticky dough.
3. Knead gently on a lightly floured surface and shape mixture into 10 balls. Place well apart on a lightly greased baking sheet.
4. Brush with a little milk to glaze then bake in a hot oven, 200°C/400°F/gas mark 6 for about 20 minutes until golden brown and bases sound hollow when tapped.

Prep time: 10 minutes
Cook time: 20 minutes

All-in-One Cake

makes 1 x 18 cm/7 in cake

ingredients	Metric	Imperial	American
Self-raising (self-rising) flour	175 g	6 oz	1½ cups
Baking powder	5 ml	1 tsp	1 tsp
Caster (superfine) sugar	175 g	6 oz	¾ cup
Soft margarine	175 g	6 oz	¾ cup
Eggs	3	3	3
To finish:			
Jam, a little extra caster (superfine) sugar			

method

1. Put all ingredients in a processor and run machine just until mixture is blended and smooth, or put in a bowl and beat with a wooden spoon for about two minutes until smooth. DO NOT OVER BEAT.

2. Grease two 18 cm/7 in sandwich tins (pans) and line bases with baking parchment. Divide mixture between tins and level surfaces.

3. Bake in a moderately hot oven, 190°C/375°F/gas mark 5 for 20 minutes until risen, golden and centres spring back when pressed. Turn out onto a wire rack to cool. Remove paper.

4. Sandwich together with jam and sprinkle with a little caster sugar.

Prep time: 10 minutes
Cook time: 20 minutes

variations

CHOCOLATE: Substitute 25 g/1 oz/2 tbsp of flour with cocoa (unsweetened chocolate) powder. Fill with whipped cream or chocolate spread.

COFFEE: Dissolve 15 g/1 tbsp instant coffee granules in 15 ml/1 tbsp water, add to basic mix. Sandwich with sweetened cream, flavoured with coffee liqueur or 5 ml/1 tsp coffee granules dissolved in 5 ml/1 tsp water.

Crispy Oatcake Thins

Perfect for breakfast spread with butter and jam or marmalade, or to serve with cheese.

makes 8

ingredients	Metric	Imperial	American
Medium oatmeal	75 g	3 oz	¾ cup
Salt			
Bicarbonate of soda (baking soda)	1.5 ml	¼ tsp	¼ tsp
Butter, melted	15 g	½ oz	1 tbsp
Hot water	60 ml	4 tbsp	4 tbsp
Oil for greasing			

method

1. Put all ingredients except oil in a bowl and mix to a dough.
2. Turn out on a surface dusted with oatmeal and pat or roll out thinly to about a 25 cm/10 in round.
3. Cut out 8 wedges.
4. Lightly oil a large frying pan (skillet) and heat gently.
5. Cook oatcakes a few at a time until firm. Turn over carefully so they don't break and cook for 2 - 3 minutes more. Cool on a wire rack. Store in an airtight tin.

Prep time: 10 minutes
Cook time: 3 - 5 minutes

EASY-DOES-IT BISCUITS

makes about 20

ingredients	Metric	Imperial	American
Soft butter or margarine	65 g	2½ oz	5 tbsp
Caster (superfine) sugar	50 g	2 oz	¼ cup
Vanilla essence (extract)	5 ml	1 tsp	1 tsp
Self-raising (self-rising) flour	100 g	4 oz	1 cup
To decorate:			
Whole blanched almonds or Glacé (candied) cherries, halved			

method

1. Put all ingredients in a processor and run machine until mixture just forms a ball. OR put in a bowl and work with a fork or wooden spoon until mixture forms a ball.

2. Shape into walnut-sized balls and place a little apart on a greased baking sheet (you may need two). Press down with a fork dipped in cold water.

3. Bake in a moderately hot oven, 190°C/375°F/gas mark 5 for about 15 minutes until pale golden. Top each immediately with a nut or cherry half and leave for a few minutes to harden then transfer to a wire rack to cool.

Prep time: 10 - 15 minutes
Cook time: 15 minutes

Muesli Cookies

makes about 30

ingredients

	Metric	Imperial	American
Margarine	75 g	3 oz	1/3 cup
Soft brown sugar	75 g	3 oz	1/3 cup
Golden (light corn) syrup	20 ml	4 tsp	4 tsp
Bicarbonate of soda (baking soda)	5 ml	1 tsp	1 tsp
Plain (all-purpose) flour	75 g	3 oz	3/4 cup
Muesli	150 g	5 oz	1 cup

method

1. Melt margarine, sugar and syrup in a pan. Add bicarbonate of soda - it will froth up.

2. Stir in the flour and muesli. Shape into walnut sized balls and place a little apart on two greased baking sheets. Flatten slightly with a fork.

3. Bake in a moderately hot oven 190°C/375°F/gas mark 5 for 8 - 10 minutes or until golden brown. Leave to cool for 2 minutes, then transfer to a wire rack to cool completely.

Prep time: 10 - 15 minutes
Cook time: 8 - 10 minutes

No-Bake Chocolate Fudge Cake

ingredients	Metric	Imperial	American
Butter or margarine	100 g	4 oz	½ cup
Icing (confectioners') sugar	175 g	6 oz	¾ cup
Cocoa (unsweetened chocolate) powder	15 ml	1 tbsp	1 tbsp
Small chocolate fudge finger bars, cut in pieces	3	3	3
Plain sweet biscuits (cookies), crushed	175 g	6 oz	1½ cups
Mixed nuts, chopped	50 g	2 oz	½ cup
To decorate:			
A little sifted icing (confectioners') sugar			

method

1. Put butter, sugar, cocoa and fudge fingers in a pan and heat gently, stirring until melted.

2. Add biscuits and nuts and mix well.

3. Turn into a greased 18 cm/7 in square sandwich tin (pan) and press down well. Leave to cool then chill until set. Turn out onto a serving plate, dust with icing sugar and serve cut in fingers or squares.

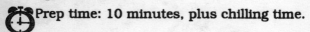
Prep time: 10 minutes, plus chilling time.

Peanut Honey Bites

These biscuits make a quick and delicious tea-time treat.

makes 12

ingredients	Metric	Imperial	American
Butter or margarine	75 g	3 oz	1/3 cup
Set honey	45 ml	3 tbsp	3 tbsp
Plain biscuits (cookies), crushed	225 g	8 oz	2 cups
Grated lemon rind	5 ml	1 tsp	1 tsp
Crunchy peanut butter	45 ml	3 tbsp	3 tbsp

method

1. Melt fat with honey and bring to the boil.
2. Stir in remaining ingredients and mix well.
3. Press into a greased 18 cm/7 in square sandwich tin and chill until set. Cut into squares before serving.

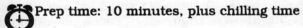 Prep time: 10 minutes, plus chilling time

RUM TRUFFLE CAKES

These truffle cakes are perfect to serve with coffee after dinner, but are irresistible any time.

makes 12

ingredients	Metric	Imperial	American
Golden (light corn) syrup	30 ml	2 tbsp	2 tbsp
Butter	25 g	1 oz	2 tbsp
Cocoa (unsweetened chocolate) powder	30 ml	2 tbsp	2 tbsp
Plain cake crumbs	100 g	4 oz	2 cups
Icing (confectioners') sugar	15 ml	1 tbsp	1 tbsp
Rum essence (extract)			
To decorate:			
Cocoa (unsweetened chocolate) powder			

method

1. Melt syrup, butter and cocoa powder together. Stir in cake crumbs, sugar and a few drops of rum essence to taste. Roll into 12 small balls. Chill for about 20 minutes then roll in cocoa powder and place in paper cases. Store in the fridge.

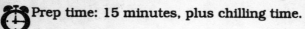
Prep time: 15 minutes, plus chilling time.

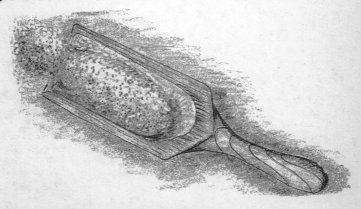

INDEX

anchovies
  whiting with cheese and anchovies 67
apples
  blackberry and apple layer 148
  caramel apples 149
apricots
  Greek yoghurt surprise 156
artichokes
  Brittany artichokes 26
Asian pears with blue cheese mayonnaise 22
asparagus
  asparagus with fresh herb hollandaise 23
aubergines
  aubergine dip 24
Austrian pork chops 95
avocados
  avocado South American-style 25
  bacon egg and avocado salad 96-7
  cottage avocado 29

bacon
  bacon egg and avocado salad 96-7
  liver with bacon and onion sauce 84
  macaroni masterpiece 136
  spaghetti with bacon and eggs 105
  sticky orange steaks 106
bananas
  bananas with hot lemon butter sauce 146
  Caribbean bananas 147
barbecued pork 98
beef
  beef and noodle stir-fry 69
  burgundy-style steak 70
  fillet steaks Wyrardisbury 71
  minute steak Diane 72
  popovers 75
  salt beef and potato salad 77
  see also minced beef
biscuits
  easy-does-it biscuits 182
  see also cookies
blackberries
  blackberry and apple layer 148

bread
  garlic bread 173
  herby pittas 174
  hot walnut bread 175
  pitta pocket cooler 140
  quick cheese soda bread 177
  savoury wholemeal rolls 179
Brittany artichokes 26
broccoli
  broccoli and ham au gratin 99

Caesar salad special 121
cakes
  all-in-one cake 180
  no-bake chocolate fudge cake 184
calamares à la plancha 27
caramel apples 149
cashew nuts
  Chinese-style chicken with cashew nuts 113
cheese
  Asian pears with blue cheese mayonnaise 22
  broccoli and ham au gratin 99
  cheese soda bread 177
  cheesy chicken topper 109
  fondue 142
  golden camembert with cranberry sauce 34
  golden cheddar soup 11
  Mozzarella and tomatoes with basil 40
  soda bread 177
  Somerset rarebit 142
  whiting with cheese and anchovies 67
  see also cottage cheese
cheesecake *see* desserts
chicken
  cheesy chicken topper 109
  chicken and coconut Masala 110
  chicken in filo pastry 111
  chicken Hawaii 112
  chicken stroganoff 104
  Chinese-style chicken with cashew nuts 113
  crunchy chicken escalopes 114
  fragrant chicken livers 116

Spanish rice 118
chilli, quick chilli 76
Chinese style salad 28
chocolate
   all-in-one cake 180
   chocolate mousse 151
   chocolate-dipped delights 150
   no-bake chocolate fudge cake 184
clementines
   melon and clementine cocktail 37
coconut
   chicken and coconut Masala 110
cod
   cod provençale 55
   see also smoked cod
coffee
   all-in-one cake 180
   coffee cream cheese italienne 152
cookies
   muesli cookies 183
cornmeal pancakes 172
cottage cheese
   cottage avocado 29
   pineapple boats 44
crab
   creamy cucumber with crab 30-1
cream cheese
   coffee cream cheese italienne 152
croissants 137
croque madame 134
cucumber
   chilled cucumber soup with dill 9
   creamy cucumber with crab 30-1
   cucumber and potato gourmet 122
curried parsnip soup 10

desserts
   bananas with hot lemon butter sauce 146
   blackberry and apple layer 148
   caramel apples 149
   Caribbean bananas 147
   chocolate mousse 151
   chocolate-dipped delights 150
   coffee cream cheese italienne 152
   fresh fruit platter with raspberry sauce 153
   frinklies 154
   fruit brulée 155
   Greek yoghurt surprise 156
   jalousie 157
   lemon dream 158
   mango fool 159
   melon glacé 160
   minted melon and raspberries 161
   orange raffles 162
   pear and ginger strudels 163
   pink grapefruit cheesecake 164
   sparkling nectarines 165
   strawberry and peach Romanoff 166
   strawberry syllabub 167
   toffee plum charlotte 168
   tropicana delight 169
   Zabaglione 170
dips
   aubergine dip 24
   Brittany artichokes 26
dressings
   Chinese style salad 28
   pears with creamy tarragon dressing 43
   smoked mackerel with horseradish mayonnaise 47
duck
   duck breasts à l'orange 115

eggs
   bacon egg and avocado salad 96-7
   Greek egg and lemon soup 12
   jellied eggs en cocotte 35
   rosy eggs 45
   saucy ham 'n eggs 141
   spaghetti with bacon and eggs 105

fegattini (meatballs) 102
filo pastry
   chicken in filo pastry 111
   pizza parcels 126
   salmon parcels 60-1
fish
   baked stuffed plaice 53
   buttery mackerel 54
   calamares à la plancha 27
   Chinese style salad 28

cod provençale 55
fish creole 56
fish and potato fry 57
hearty fish stew 58
quick kedgeree 59
salmon parcels 60-1
saucy smoked mackerel 62
smoked mackerel with horseradish
    mayonnaise 47
smoked salmon pâté 48
swordfish steaks paysanne 63
tandoori fish 64-5
tangy whiting goujons 50
trout in soured cream 66
tuna steaks paysanne 63
whiting with cheese and anchovies 67
see also shellfish
fondue
　cheese fondue 142
fruit
　fresh fruit platter with raspberry sauce
      153
　fruit brulée 155

gammon
　deluxe grill 100
　gammon and potato salad 77
garlic
　garlic bread 173
　garlicky mushrooms 33
ginger
　pear and ginger strudels 163
grapefruit
　pink grapefruit cheesecake 164
　royal grapefruit 46
Greek egg and lemon soup 12
Greek yoghurt surprise 156
Greek-style lamb kebabs 82

haddock, see smoked haddock
ham
　broccoli and ham au gratin 99
　cheesy chicken topper 109
　melon with Westphalian ham 38
　saucy ham 'n eggs 141
hollandaise sauce 23, 60

kebabs
　Greek-style lamb kebabs 82
kedgeree 59
kidneys
　devilled kidneys 101
　tiddley kidneys 93

lamb
　eastern lamb 81
　Greek-style lamb kebabs 82
　lemon glazed cutlets 83
　Rosie's cutlets 88
　saucy lamb with capers 90-1
　Somerset lamb 92
　see also minced lamb
lemon
　Greek egg and lemon soup 12
　lemon dream 158
　lemon glazed cutlets 83
liver
　fegattini 102
　fragrant chicken livers 116
　liver with bacon and onion sauce 84

macaroni
　macaroni masterpiece 136
mackerel
　buttery mackerel 54
　see also smoked mackerel
mangoes
　mango fool 159
mayonnaise
　horseradish mayonnaise 47
meat see named varieties of meat
meatballs
　fegattini 102
Mediterranean summer soup 14
melon
　melon and clementine cocktail 37
　melon glacé 160
　melon with Westphalian ham 38
　minted melon and raspberries 161
minced beef
　pasta grill 73
　pied-à-terre pie 74
　quick chilli 76
　quick moussaka 86-7

minced lamb
  quick moussaka 86-7
minestrone 18
minted melon and raspberries 161
minted pea soup 15
Moorish mushrooms 36
moules marinière 39
moussaka 86-7
mousse, chocolate mousse 151
Mozzarella and tomatoes with basil 40
muesli cookies 183
mushrooms
  devilled mushrooms 135
  Moorish mushrooms 36
  mushroom and corn chowder 16
  mushroom pâté 41
  spaghetti with turkey and mushrooms 117
mussels
  moules marinière 39

nectarines
  chocolate-dipped delights 150
  fruit brulée
  sparkling nectarines 165
noodles
  beef and noodle stir-fry 69

oatmeal
  crispy oatcake thins 181
oranges
  orange raffles 162

pancakes
  cornmeal pancakes 172
  rye Scotch pancakes 178
pasta
  macaroni masterpiece 136
  minced beef pasta grill 73
  pasta grill 73
  spaghetti with bacon and eggs 105
  spaghetti with green herbs and mushrooms 129
  spaghetti with turkey and mushrooms 117
pastry *see* filo pastry; puff pastry

pâté
  mushroom pâté 41
  pâté-stuffed peppers 42
  peppers stuffed with 42
  smoked salmon pâté 48
peaches
  chocolate-dipped delights 150
  fruit brulée 155
  strawberry and peach Romanoff 166
peanuts
  peanut soup 17
pears
  Asian pears with blue cheese mayonnaise 22
  pear and ginger strudels 163
  pears with creamy tarragon dressing 43
peppers
  pâté-stuffed peppers 42
pies
  pied-à-terre pie 74
pineapples
  chicken Hawaii 112
  pineapple boats 44
  tropicana delight 169
pink grapefruit cheesecake 164
pipierade 139
pitta bread
  herby pittas 174
  pitta pocket cooler 140
pizza
  pan pizza 138
  pizza parcels 126
plaice
  baked stuffed plaice 52-3
plums
  fruit brulée 155
  toffee plum charlotte 168
pork
  Austrian pork chops 95
  barbecued pork 98
  crunchy pork escalopes 114
  oriental pork slices 103
  pork stroganoff 104
  sticky orange steaks 106
  see also bacon; gammon; ham

potatoes
    cucumber and potato gourmet 122
    fish and potato fry 57
    salt beef or gammon and potato
        salad 77
    spicy potato cakes 143
    tortilla 144
prawns
    Chinese style salad 28
    creamy cucumber with prawns 31-2
puff pastry
    jalousie 157

raspberries
    fresh fruit platter with raspberry
        sauce 153
    fruit brulée 155
    minted melon and raspberries 161
ratatouille 123
rice
    Greek egg and lemon soup 12
    regatta rice ring 127
    Spanish rice 118
roulades
    watercress roulade 130
runner beans
    sweet'n sour runner beans 49
rye Scotch pancakes 178

salads
    bacon egg and avocado salad 96-7
    Caesar salad special 121
    Chinese style salad 28
    salt beef and potato salad 77
    Sicilian salad 128
salmon
    salmon parcels 60-1
    see also smoked salmon
sauces
    hollandaise sauce 23, 60
    hot lemon butter sauce 146
    raspberry sauce 153
    soured cream sauce 66
    watercress sauce 141
shellfish
    Chinese style salad 28

creamy cucumber with crab or prawns
    30-1
moules marinière 39
Sicilian salad 128
smoked cod, quick kedgeree 59
smoked haddock, quick kedgeree 59
smoked mackerel
    saucy smoked mackerel 62
    smoked mackerel with horseradish
        mayonnaise 47
smoked salmon
    smoked salmon pâté 48
snacks and light meals
    croque madame 134
    devilled mushrooms 135
    macaroni masterpiece 136
    melting crescents 137
    pan pizza 138
    pipierade 139
    pitta pocket cooler 140
    saucy ham 'n eggs 141
    Somerset rarebit 142
    spicy potato cakes 143
    tortilla 144
soups
    bortsch 8
    chilled cucumber soup with dill 9
    curried parsnip soup 10
    golden cheddar soup 11
    Greek egg and lemon soup 12
    green velvet soup 13
    Mediterranean summer soup 14
    minted pea soup 15
    mushroom and corn chowder 16
    peanut soup 17
    quick minestrone 18
    watercress soup 19
spaghetti
    spaghetti with bacon and eggs 105
    spaghetti with green herbs and
        mushrooms 129
    spaghetti with turkey and mushrooms
        117
Spanish rice 118
squid
    calamares à la plancha 27

starters
  Asian pears with blue cheese mayonnaise 22
  asparagus with fresh herb hollandaise 23
  aubergine dip 24
  avocado South American-style 25
  Brittany artichokes 26
  calamares à la plancha 27
  Chinese style salad 28
  cottage avocado 29
  creamy cucumber with crab 30-1
  garlicky mushrooms 33
  golden camembert with cranberry sauce 34
  jellied eggs en cocotte 35
  melon and clementine cocktail 37
  melon with Westphalian ham 38
  moorish mushrooms 36
  moules marinière 39
  mozzarella and tomatoes with basil 40
  mushroom pâté 41
  pâté-stuffed peppers 42
  pears with creamy tarragon dressing 43
  pineapple boats 44
  rosy eggs 45
  royal grapefruit 46
  smoked mackerel with horseradish mayonnaise 47
  smoked salmon pâté 48
  spicy potato cakes 143
  sweet'n sour runner beans 49
  tandoori fish 64-5
  tangy whiting goujons 50
strawberries
  fruit brulée 155
  strawberry and peach Romanoff 166
  strawberry syllabub 167
sweetcorn
  cornmeal pancakes 172
  mushroom and corn chowder 16
swordfish
  swordfish steaks paysanne 63

toffee plum charlotte 168

tomatoes
  Mozzarella and tomatoes with basil 40
tortilla 144
tripe
  tripe Romanov 78
trout
  trout in soured cream 66
tuna
  Chinese style salad 28
  tuna steaks paysanne 63
turkey
  crunchy turkey escalopes 114
  spaghetti with turkey and mushrooms 117

vegetables
  bortsch 8
  Caesar salad special 121
  cucumber and potato gourmet 122
  golden cheddar soup 11
  hearty fish stew 58
  Mediterranean summer soup 14
  no-nonsense ratatouille 123
  pissaladiere 124-5
  pizza parcels 126
  quick minestrone 18
  regatta rice ring 127
  spaghetti with green herbs and mushrooms 129
  watercress roulade 130-1

walnuts
  hot walnut bread 175
watercress
  watercress roulade 130-1
  watercress sauce 141
  watercress soup 19
whiting
  with cheese and anchovies 67
  tangy whiting goujons 50

yams
  curried yam soup 10
yoghurt
  Greek yoghurt surprise 156

Zabaglione 170